Buffalo Morgan's Sowing the Sacred Seeds of Sanity

Sick & Funny Comedy from Buffalo's Vegas Show

Barry Hemmerle

Editing by Amy Lignor

Book 3

DEDICATION

This book is dedicated to everybody with something to say who can express it through whatever artistic form they choose.

I also want to give a great deal of credit to my son, Dan. His opinions of my writing help keep me focused on making my books as entertaining as possible.

I'm also bringing a new illustrator into the Morgan family. Juan Cabrera is a true friend and a real talent with a wonderful imagination. Thank you, Juan!

Also...a big "HELLO" goes out to my first grandchild, Jason Hemmerle. You are most definitely allowed to read this...when you turn 30.

Buffalo Morgan's Sowing the Seeds of Sanity

Sick & Funny Comedy from Buffalo's Vegas
Show
By Barry Hemmerle

For more books like this one, visit Barry Hemmerle's
website at:
http://barryhemmerle.com/

Printed in the United States of America
The publisher offers discounts on this book when
ordered in bulk quantities. For more information,
contact Sales Department, Phone 815-290-9605,
Email:
sales@FreedomOfSpeechPublishing.com

Product and company names mentioned herein are the
trademarks or registered trademarks of their respective
owners.

Freedom of Speech Publishing, Leawood KS, 66224
www.FreedomOfSpeechPublishing.com

ISBN: 1938634128
ISBN-13: 978-1-938634-12-3

A SPECIAL THANK YOU TO YOU!

On behalf of everyone at Freedom Of Speech Publishing, thank you for choosing Buffalo Morgan's Sowing the Seeds of Sanity: Sick & Funny Comedy from Buffalo's Vegas Show for your reading enjoyment.

As an added bonus and special thank you, for purchasing Buffalo Morgan's Sowing the Seeds of Sanity: Sick & Funny Comedy from Buffalo's Vegas Show, you can enjoy discounts and special promotions on other Freedom of Speech Publishing products. Visit www.freedomeofspeech.com/vip to learn more.

We are committed to providing you with the highest level of customer satisfaction possible. If for any reason you have questions or comments, we are delighted to hear from you. Email us at cs@freedomofspeechpublishing.com or visit our website at: http://freedomofspeechpublishing.com/contact-us-2/.

If you enjoyed Buffalo Morgan's Sowing the Seeds of Sanity: Sick & Funny Comedy from Buffalo's Vegas Show, visit www.freedomofspeechpublishing.com for a list of similar books
or upcoming books.

Again, thank you for your patronage. We look forward to providing you more entertainment in the future.

Contents

ACKNOWLEDGMENTS

To the folks that helped me this time around , I give a heartfelt thanks... They are, Dan H., Amy L., Juan the Artist, Patrick K., Ted P., the creators of FIREBALL and the farmers that grow my food and weed.....

Thank you, EVERYBODY...

Introduction

When you go to a play, you pretty much know what you're going to receive; and when it comes to live entertainment, that's a whole lot of input.

Stand-up comedy is free. There are no rules. Comics can drink on the job, swear on the job, and talk about your mother…on the job. And as long as you're laughing, we're doing our job.

The only rules that are the same in this book are: 'Pinga' means penis, scootch means vagina, and the "F" word will make a couple hundred cameos.

———

Now…direct from the Hellhole Comedy Club—for the 16th straight week—give it up for…

Buffalo Morgan!

Chapter 1:
This is My 'Bitch-Ass' Life!

"Thank you…thank you very much. Please…Please sit down. Come on now! You're making me miss one of my fringe benefits. If everybody's standing up, I can't look down this charming young lady's shirt sitting in the front row.

Hello Baaaaaby! How'd you like to get married?? No? Okay…come back next month when you're a little more desperate

You're married…to him? Christ, look at the size of him! Uh, these are just jokes. I'm not really looking at your wife's big, juicy…perfectly shaped…natural looking…uh, piece of…yummy. Don't kill me, dude!

Can a waitress please bring a pitcher of Mai Tai's to table 2?

I'm very sorry, sir. I should have been a mime. I apologize to you, your wife…and her fun bags.

2

That's why most males decide to become comics, by the way. The money sucks and the health benefits are non-existent, but if I can look down a shirt or two, it makes this poor career choice seem almost tolerable. Yeah, we love to make girls like you laugh...hysterically. Then I get an unrelenting urge to go out and do Jello shots.

You're a lucky man, sir. Look at her beautiful face...her incredible body. Tell us the truth...she's a real bitch at home right?? No? Damnit! Does she snort? You know, when she laughs like—Ha Ha Ha—SNORT! No? She looks like a snorter if you ask me. I love snorters. It's like knocking them off their pedestal. And all of a sudden...I have a chance. That's when the shark comes out.

Hey, how about a bet? You say your wife is not a snorter; I say I can get her to snort. Here you go, if I can get your wife to snort then...I can have casual sex with her. No, really, hear me out. It will be *so* casual she may not even know it happened.

I am quick. I might be done before she undresses. Now, hold on… If I can't get her to snort then you win.

What do you win? What is this, 'Let's Make a Deal?' Are you actually considering this, sir? You better say no.

But what *do* you win? Wow, this dude is just screaming for a divorce, people.

Okay, your prize is, you don't have to kick my ass.

Thank you…Thank you all for coming. Welcome to the HELLHOLE. Why there's a flashing neon light that says 'HELLHOLE', I'll never know. All you have to do is stick your head in the door and the image of a major HELLHOLE comes immediately to mind, along with a gallon of gas and some matches.

That's what most comedy clubs are.

When they are new, they are fancy restaurants. Then, when they hit middle age, they become fast food joints. Then, a few years before the wrecking ball comes in to take them out, you have the death trap in which you are seated now. But, fuck it, it's only a building.

———

I get so tired hearing people cry about how tough life can be. If you're not happy, do something that makes you happy. Everything has a silver lining. You have to look for it.

Poverty…Trust me, I know about this one: I'm poor. It sucks, but here are some silver linings:

My TV: It's a half-ton Panoramasaurus from the mid 70's. Any burglar with 5 years of flat screen theft experience under his belt would get a hernia just thinking about getting that fucker down the steps. Now *that's* security of mind.

My computer's old. In the back it has jacks for telegraph wires. The closest I get to porn on my computer is if I use a copy of *Playboy* to level out the table.

The only burglars that would steal my crap would have to be into nostalgia or antiques. And if it's not old, it's fake. You know how people have fruit bowls with—you know—fruit in them and some folks put artificial fruit in them? I have a picture of fruit in mine…may have come with it. That's probably how I knew it was a fruit bowl. See? *Silver lining*.

Things are going good now. When you work yourself out of poverty, everything else just kind of falls in line. Funny how money works.

I feel good, but every once in a while my mind misses not being under stress. I have anxiety attacks because I can't deal with not being stressed. I walk around my house waiting for the walls to cave in on me. Know what I use for a cure? I mean, besides pot? I'll watch the news for an hour.

My blood pressure jumps off the chart and the stress just wraps itself around me like a cheap blanket. "Ooohh… that's good."

———

Do we really need the news anymore? I don't mean weather or traffic. That we need. Topless weather girls would be better. Wish I controlled the media. Yeah, I know, that's sexist. But it's also kind of funny, you know, from a guy's point of view.

There's a lot of stuff men don't know about women and I think men just don't want to know.

Here's an example…

Women can get hernias. It's true. I haven't a clue how a doctor would check them though. Unless they have their husband's cookies in their purse, the standard test is pretty useless. If a doctor asks you to turn your head and cough, he probably just wants to watch your boobs shake.

Women have wet dreams. It's true. But they don't have to clean the sheets the next day. They just wake up in a great freakin mood.

———

Say…did you ever find yourself not being able to extract yourself out of a conversation that you don't feel like having?

It happened to me tonight before I got here. I stopped off at a convenience store for my lottery tickets. *I GOTS to have my tickets!* So this old Indian dude just starts talking away like he sucked down a case of 5-hour energy drinks. He was totally jacked up. But he had this crazy smile on him that was a cross between; 'my bitch wife left me' and 'I have been inhaling the best shit of my life'.

I couldn't walk away. I wanted to say, "Um, I am understanding every sixth word and I have a sold-out show waiting for me." But I couldn't; for 20 minutes I was held verbally hostage. And I still don't know what he said. I just nodded a lot. That seemed to make him happy.

It's hard to be cool in that situation.

———

I bet you guys don't know how hard it is to be *this* cool. It takes up a lot of my day. My first thought in the morning is: "What can I do for my fans today to prove I'm cool?" Nah…I'm just fuckin with you.

The world can spin as fast as it wants, but I'm gonna chill over here. But when I see the revolution starting, I'm running to the head of the line. I don't want to start the damn thing if, when I storm an embassy, I'm all by myself. Boy, would I feel like an ass.

The one trait I have that I consider 'uncool' is the fact I still get starstruck. Then I need time to work through it and I'm fine.

A big moment in my life was meeting The Beach Boys. But I had a day to prepare for it. My agent called me one night to talk business. At the end of the call he tells me to wear a nice shirt tomorrow and he'll pick me up at eight.

So I say, "Where we going tomorrow?"

He says, and I quote: "We're going to The Beach Boys concert. A couple guys in the band want to meet you."

Two minutes later, I still got my phone up to my ear, *"What?* What the fuck did you say?"

I got 24-hours to get myself in mental shape to meet these guys. So the whole next day, like someone in an asylum, I'm walking around my hotel room imagining I'm with The Beach Boys shaking their imaginary hands, "Great job on the Pet Sound album."

So when I went to meet them, I was cool. I also had my people film this historic meeting. What? I HAVE people!

I have to be ready!

Now, 4 years later, I'm in Seattle in an antiques store and I look up and there's Johnny Depp; he's standing closer to me then you are. I nearly pulled his arm out of its socket shaking his hand, pledging my eternal friendship to him, and also throwing out a bad impression of him from 'Pirates of the Caribbean.'

"That's CAPTAIN…Jack Sparrow." And someone filmed that meeting too. Guess which video went viral on YouTube?? Can you guess???

See, it takes work to be cool. Even when I write poetry…it's cool. Here's a cute little Christmas one for you to gnaw on:

Mrs. Claus (a.k.a. The Ice Bitch)

Jingle, Jingle, the Christmas bells. The roof is made for docking;

Redheads, blondes, and brunettes too. I'll fill more than their stocking.

Surprises down the chimney chute.

My, what a beautiful tree and a redhead full of silicone. "Good lord, are those for me?"

A gentle nod, her eyes twinkled, and there was a sofa by the fire.

"Let me take this damn suit off and I'll show you something to admire."

The belt is gone and so are the pants. No, I don't use underwear.

11

Her horrified look made me look down at the cashew hanging there...

I finished my night and raced back home, slamming the door behind me.

"Did you find the Salt Peter?" she said.

"I put it in your coffee."

———

I wrote 2 books of poetry. It's very rock-and-roll. I can't write.

"And a unicorn burst through the rainbow."

Get the hell out of here! If I write a poem about unicorns and rainbows, it would probably go like this: "As I strangle the last unicorn with a rainbow, my buddy beat it with a board."

Paint one hell of a picture, don't I?

How bout vigilantism? Everybody likes hero stories.

Drugs and alcohol...Most guys like one or the other...or both...

Why you staring at me? Did something fall out of my pocket?

Different journeys of the mind: Everything from sipping a Budweiser to licking a toad can be had by the really choosy ones.

———

I won an award last year for a piece I wrote describing the joy of divorce. I think it was called, "The Joy of Divorce." I describe it as 'I got my soul and my reason to live back'.

There are some people that should never divorce. Like ugly people…if you had a hard time landing a mate at the altar, or even just getting laid, you may just want to stick with what you got. Work out your little problems, because 9 times out of 10, you didn't improve with age.

Many people work really hard in a marriage and make it look easy, but it's a house of cards. It's almost like a staring contest…

Him: "I love you."

Her: "I love you."

Him: "I love you."

Her: "You blinked! We're coming apart at the seams."

Religious people divorce too.

Me: "Hey Phil, why are you getting a divorce?"

Phil: "Because God won't kill the bitch no matter how much I pray."

I think we should screw all the divorce lawyers in the world. How, you ask? Put an expiration date on the marriage license…say 5 years. When it comes to renewal time, you sit down and see if you wanna do another 5. If not, just walk away and start anew. And don't worry about the kids…with all the iPad crap out there now they practically raise themselves.

———

I've been wanting to ask you folks, if you were gonna be a superhero who would you be? And I don't mean an established superhero, like Superman, you can't have all those powers, like the fastest and strongest; blah, blah, blah.

You get one superpower and you build your superhero from the fairy-lookin boots on up.

Know who I'd be? O-Man!

I'd spell it just the way it sounds. Can you guess what my superpower would be? Not even close. My superpower would be (*drum roll, please*) every woman I sleep with has the greatest night by *far*...

I knock her so far out of the park, she's afraid to go again but the addiction has begun. And she's afraid she may never have it that good again, so she has to jump back on.

Because... I. AM. O-Man!

I know what you're thinking, "What does this have to do with fighting crime?" Well, it *would* keep me off the streets.

Do you realize the prices I could charge once my reputation grows? *What?* You don't really think I'm above prostitution, do you? I do it now, for $20 a head, every night.

I'm raping your ears as I speak.

Because... I. AM. O-Man!

———

I still have casual sex at 50. I still even look life-like. Come back in 30 years and we'll discuss it. By then, the party should be over. Oh, yeah, I do not plan to grow old gracefully. If my relatives are any indicator, I should end up with huge ears and the skin of a crocodile.

I'm sorry if I sound a little crabby. I got pulled over again…

———

Just once I'd like to be pulled over for D.U.I. and not *be* D.U.I.

I don't really drink and drive. It's a bad idea and that's why I'm divorced…I'm a terrible liar.

So, have we all got our bucket lists together? I work toward them. I want NO regrets. I fulfilled an item last month, actually: Number 6. I wanted to have sex outside…anywhere, just outside. Bang! Knocked it off the list!

I just wish there'd been somebody there with me. I felt like a total idiot. But you'd be amazed how many people will stop what they're doing and watch you.

And with everybody talking it made it hard to concentrate and finish. Then the mood killer was when someone pointed and spoke, "Can anybody do that outside, or is he like the president of Europe."

I'm sorry. I just needed to share the pain. Let's move on...

———

Know what you don't see anymore? Globes. I was looking at one the other day and, except for America, I don't know where jackshit is anymore.

"Canada's attached to us??"

"Arctic...Arctic...Antarctica...damnit!"

"When did England become an island?"

I *did* know where Panama and Columbia were, but that's because as a teen I wanted to know where my weed came from.

I feel if my teachers really had wanted to reach me, they would have incorporated certain aspects of my unique personality into the daily lesson.

Teacher: "Todd went to his dealer's house and purchased 10 pounds of high grade California sensimilla. When he got it home, he broke it down into ounces. How many ounces did he have? Mr....Morgan?"

Buffalo: "160 ounces, sir. Unless Todd's dealer was my dealer, then he only had 158."

I loved high school. It really was cool and the teachers loved me...well, loved, loathed – same dif. I knew that didn't sound right. But they only had a loathing because I sucked. Just lazy. In gym class the only way I'd run around the track was if the teacher dressed like a cop. I stole scales, rubber tubing and beakers from Science class, so it was a real 'early' form of all those stupid games like, Grand Theft Auto.

One time I sold a kid a 20-dollar bag of chalk dust. Funny? Who cares. I got the twenty bucks to buy the shit I wanted, and the kid learned a valuable life lesson. After all, isn't that what high school's for?

I think the only reason I graduated was because I have beautiful penmanship. My history teacher once told me, "Your report on Genghis Khan is the stupidest nonsense I ever read...but it was so beautifully written, PASS!"

One class I really didn't like was auto body. I was a terrible mechanic...

———

I've hated working on cars since I got my first car—a Ford P.O.S. Not that all Fords are P.O.S. but this one was. 16-years old, no backseats, (and don't ask me why because I have no idea), an oil leak that rivaled the Exxon Valdez. That's right you're not escaping history yet! You bastards killed a lot of seals...and I like seals! ...Bastards.

Anyway, my leak was *that* bad. How I fixed it? I soldered one end of a garden hose over the leak; then I circled the hose over the engine block and back into the hole where you put oil in. I know. Genius. Thank you.

I figure I probably saved about 700 quarts of oil that way…Pretty smart.

What would have been smarter, maybe, would have been to fix the freaking problem.

Tell me if any of these problems sounds familiar: Driver side door doesn't open, windshield leaks, window won't go down, window won't go up, a radiator on life support, a spare that's flat, wrong size lug wrench, a faulty gas gauge, car stalls if there's a hint of rain, occasional brakes, dead driver's side wiper, and a busted axle. These were the combined problems of my first three cars. I believe I set a record.

———

Know what I've been liking more? I like to go to casinos, but sometimes I'm just not in the mood to gamble. You see, I'm treading foreclosure slips because I've been infected with perpetual poverty. So I like to sit around and watch people blow their money. Slot players are the best. They'll rub their machine, pray to it…I've even seen old men rub up against it…you know…like a woman. And all the while they're feeding these things 20 dollar bills as fast as their bony fingers can snatch them from their fanny packs.

I work in a lot of casinos and I go into a lot of public bathrooms…it comes with the gig. I don't have a problem with that. What I do have a problem with is, when I get recognized by a dude and the admirer wants to shake my hand before he washes *his*.

I'll take 2 steps back and say, "Were you raised in the woods? Clean your hands, dude."

9 out of 10 chuckle and wash their hands. But that 10th guy…always with the attitude.

"WHAT mister funnyman? The thought of my hand touching my pinga then touching you bothers you, man?"

I say, "Yeah, dude. And if you keep walking at me, my hand is gonna touch you."

Am I wrong?? I mean, *what the fuck*, right?
And if you're coming out of a stall, DO NOT
even recognize me until you defecal your hands.
I think we're all in agreement that none of us
want someone else's fecal matter on our hands,
right? Ok? Okay.

There have been a couple times I've heard
guys giving their 5th appendage the old clean
and jerk. I don't think they knew I was there, or
else I sleep better thinking that I was invisible to
them. I'd hate to think we've devolved enough
to have sex with ourselves and want our fellow
man to hear.

But really I heard. I know what it sounds
like. I am not a child. After you hear, "Oohh
baby, yeah, jump on top, yeah," you kind of
figure he's not taking a dump and you almost
want to hear a female voice saying, "Yeah,
baby, stick it where you want to." But it never
comes. "Never the kink; always the sick."

And I'm out the door before the stall opens
up. And I don't mean the bathroom door; I'm

out the restaurant door. I am not taking a chance that he's a fan. I do not carry around that large of a container of anti-bacterial soap.

Unless I watch this guy walk out of the stall, he can be anybody in the restaurant. Some guy can come up to me and shake my hand and if I feel anything sticky, I just might pass out. It could be anything, a little honey from his toast. He was helping his daughter with a school project… But, no…my mind goes directly to public, obsessive masturbator.

Hey? Does masturbator end in O.R. or E.R.? Hey, this guy almost raised his hand. Is it clean?? Is it?

———

So anyway, this guy was looking up my ass yesterday…

Wait, that doesn't sound right.

I went to the hospital yesterday and this guy that was dressed like a doctor shoved a camera way up my back door. At least he *said* he was a doctor. Wouldn't that be funny if he wasn't? He might have been some college dude on a scavenger hunt. "Item 16: A picture of a stranger's colon."

If that's the case, I have to applaud his nerve and hope he wins. But anyway, he said I have the cleanest intestinal tract he's ever seen. Is that a compliment? Was I supposed to thank him? I'm not up on my colon etiquette.

I said it might have been that dinosaur laxative I took the other day. That hit hard. I felt a little pressure in my stomach and I thought; *Let me stroll to the bathroom.* Three steps later, I'm yelling, "Get the hell out of my way!"

Later, I did apologize to the librarian. I think there's a chemical they add to laxatives that lets you forget you took a laxative. There should be a warning on the bottle: "In 2 hours and 18 minutes, you better sit on a toilet with plungers in each hand because…it's coming…you can put a C-clamp on your flapper valve and it will still blow it off."

Since I wasn't home I was at the mercy of Fate's joke to find an unoccupied toilet. And in the library they have the single toilet bathrooms. *I might have to work fast.*

Have to tell you, I flushed a dozen mountains away...if I even thought about standing up, my ass would say: "Not a chance...blahhhhh."

After a while I had to look down to see these piles before I flushed.

One had a blue crayon in it. It had to be from 1968. But I shoved that one up my nose so he saw it all.

Upside was I had to have lost 20 pounds. I looked and felt great. But my sphincter is still trying to catch his breath. Look at this dude over here...

"Dude, did beer just come out of your nose? OH, that was sick. Glad you're having a good time."

———

I love this business. When people come up wanting to shake my hand... No, seriously...they do, I swear.

Some fans will ask me if I could repeat a joke for them and 9 out of 10 times, it's a dirty joke.

Do you have any idea how many times I've told "The Sheep Farm Joke"?? Hundreds. I hate that freakin joke. It's always the sex stuff.

And the best part for me is if I go back to the bar to get loaded, a couple of you guys will come over, we'll blow a pile of money, then I'll ask you for a sex story and, most times, it's pretty funny. I even learn stuff.

Guys, do you know what's allegedly the greatest thing to have sex with if you want the top of your head to blow off? *Got your attention now, don't I?* Sex with wet cement!" It's what I heard. I don't know. But it's what I heard. By the way, Yuck.

And the animal with a scooch closest to...well, female humans...you know...a sheep.

Don't ask me how I know it, I just do. I've never had sex with an animal unless you count my ex-wife. F.Y.B…she *knows* what it means.

———

Do you know how good it feels to be rich? No, I'm really asking you. How the hell would *I* know how money feels? The only way I can afford to see a dentist is if he has a coupon in the Yellow Pages.

What are 'Yellow Pages'? Well, young crowd, they were pages that were yellow and, uh, gave you information. One of those things…what's the word? Oh, yeah, a book.

I hate when I forget a simple word while I'm talking. I've always had that problem. One time, as a kid, it happened to me. I was going to bed. "Goodnight…uh…uh… Mom."

And I don't like forgetting stuff either. Did you ever get ready to leave your house and the little voice in your head says "STOP! You forgot something."

So I ask my inner voice; "Okay, bitch. What did I forget?" And it always says the same thing; "I ain't your bitch, dummy. And you'll have to ask another part of the brain. I'm just the 'stop' guy. I don't do any of the actual thinking."

"Bitch." By this time I forgot that I forgot something…until the voice reminds me. But what I 'forgot' forgot is really lost in the deepest crevice of my mind.

Now I don't feel like arguing with the voice again so I do the mature thing, I ignore it. So I lock the door and walk to the car. When I get there, I feel around my keyless pockets.

Now I know what I forgot. So I walk back to the house with that freakin voice going off like a teapot: "THE HOUSE KEY. It's on the same keychain as the car." But I don't listen to it until I start feeling around for my house key. Then, in synchronicity, we say, "The key is in the house."

Now I'm pissed at the voice. If it would have just told me what I forgot, I wouldn't have locked my keys in the house. So with this type of figuring, I'm never wrong.

———

I'll bet I never marry again. That is the wrong attitude to have. Ask any woman. This is how that sounds:

Me: "Hey, I'm never wrong."

She: "See, you're wrong already."

Next thing I know, I'm in front of the same divorce judge I once told: "I will never be back here again."

Oh yeah, I'm boned.

———

Do you guys like strange bets? I'm willing to bet that human males have had sex with more kinds of fish than birds. And of course, the guys deserve to be killed, but they do provide me with a bottomless pit of material.

Go ahead. Try and tell me you had sex with a chicken or a catfish. After I laugh my ass off, that's when I start asking all the juicy details. Then I want you to look me in the eye and tell me that was the best fish you ever had. Then I will quietly stop your breathing.

Yes, I live in my own little fantasy world where men can be put to death for having sex with fish. In my world, I am a god and have lots of money.

———

Do you know what's great about being rich and famous? You can do crazy things and people just say, "Oh, my, you're so eccentric."

People just figure it's one of the dozens of fringe benefits that comes along with fame. Bizarre behavior is expected. If I took a tie and used it as a bandana on Monday then by Friday, I'll see half-a-dozen other guys doing it.

Well, not me. I'm not "rich and famous." I'm, *working my way up to poverty* and "Do I know that guy?" famous. But I heard the bizarre behavior thing from people who actually pay their bills on time...lucky bastards. Rich people...don't you hate them?

I met this one dude who had truckloads of money. He didn't work; he sat around in his mansion not knowing what to do. And he's complaining. You probably know what my initial thought was, right? "Can I kill this guy and just assume his life without anyone noticing?" That's normal, right? To throw some weight on my side of the scale he was an ass and a drama queen. Does that help my case?

No? Fine, let the world be run by idiots.

———

The Brain That Went on Vacation

One of my favorite expressions is: "The Higher the Altitude, the Better the Altitude."

Guys...ever drink too much and your pinga craps out for the night? I call it S.T.S. – Star Trek Syndrome.

"We're losing power Captain and I don't know why."

"We'll fix it, Scott."

"Captain, might I suggest those last 6 shots of Jack Daniels resulted in equipment failure?"

"Spock, shut the fuck up. Bones, can he be saved?"

"Damnit Jim! I'm a pinga not a doctor."

Probably everyone knows what it's like being drunk, right? Sure you do. It's fun. But a lot of people don't know what it's like getting a good marijuana buzz. I'm sure a lot of you don't know there are different kinds of marijuana; different smells and strengths.

You didn't know that? Well, pull up a martini and have a listen. Where should I start? *Wow.*

Okay, here you go. There's a kind of marijuana that is called "Creeper" weed. You might not feel anything for like 10 minutes, but then you start to hear that voice in your head; "Sup Holmes. Sorry I took so long. Bet you thought you bought Oregano…again man, that was funny…wait, no it wasn't."

Yeah, you get a voice when you get high. And it's usually pretty funny. For a while, mine sounded like Herman Munster. Now it's matured into Peter Lorre.

I rarely do drugs anymore; I say rarely because if there's someone here with a carload of dope and in need of a good friend, I'd hate to be burning bridges. Drugs are expensive…well, except L.S.D. You do $10 of acid and walk around 'Toys R Us' it's like a Disney vacation. One time Yogi Bear was chasing me, screaming, "It's the Ranger, BooBoo!" and I'm yelling, "I'm a picnic basket, help me!"

I now have more sedate hobbies, like feeding the neighbor's dog ex-lax, giving blood, and going to the bar. Know what I really like doing? Going to confession and lying: Lielielielielie.

"Oh Holy Father, this week I watched 1,000,000 B.C. with Raquel Welch and I handled myself in an unholy manner…5 times."

Ever go to confession and forget where you are? Thought I was in the booth at one of them porn houses once and began digging for quarters.

Have you ever willfully destroyed the morals of another human being, specifically middle-aged women, marijuana-'ly' speaking? I am not afraid to play the aphrodisiac card.

By the time I finish talking about how deviate sweetly enhances sins of the flesh, we're already stoned, flying by third base and heading for home.

———

When I was a black-out drunk, the next morning I was wondering if I slept with whoever I found myself spooning with at that moment. If I'm high and the rest of the scenario is the same, there's usually one scene of hardcore chiseled into my head. That is for the future in case you're not in it…you dig?

I might not remember what you looked like when we had dinner. And I won't remember what you looked like at the movies, but I *will* remember what you looked like on all fours. And no, that doesn't make me a bad person.

And I'm not talking relationship-wise. I mean a three-day fling. You stop and say 'hello' to someone and within 5 minutes, you regret saying 'hello'.

———

Did you ever get so high you spilled your pot all over the shag carpet and then crawled around trying to salvage what you could? NO?? Me either. But I can imagine how frustrating it would be picking through the shag…pulling out hairs and chip crumbs. *God, I really need a vacuum.*

So I'm in a supermarket check-out line waiting for an old lady to go through her pockets, looking for her 10 cent coupon for suppositories for the 8th time. I start reading one of those exploit rags and they claim our President, when he was in college, loved to smoke pot. THAT...I found interesting.

So Mr. Obama...Sir...please, just legalize it! Legalize the fuck out of it. Door's already open, man. States are comin on board, so if you can hear my voice, go ahead and do it. You're into your second term so this is it. Do it! I will personally kill anyone that tries to impeach you for this. Here, Sir, here's a pen.

———

You know what I know? I don't know everything. Yeah, can you *believe* it? Weird things like...what does *enlightenment* mean? And if your first thought was 'to be enlightened', then get out of here.

No. Really. Get the fuck out.

What do you see? How do you feel? Is sex better? Come on now, you know I had to throw that out there.

Is it like the 'Matrix'? A bunch of neon green numbers. That would suck. I would miss boobies. How about you only see the good in people and everybody has big puppy dog eyes.

It's more than just idle conversation that I should ask that question. A friend of mine said it was a lot like getting high...so, you know, I took up meditation. I keep asking myself when I'm meditating, "Am I high yet? Do I feel anything?"

Someone told me that the minute I stop worrying about feeling high, I'll get enlightened faster.

"Stop worrying about feeling high?" This is gonna take a very long time. I may as well go back to cooking class...that's right, cooking class. I make the best munchies.

Here's another enlightenment question. If you get 'high' from meditating, do you get the munchies also? It's kind of an important question. It might tip the scale for me to keep taking classes.

Right now I'm thinking about chucking the classes and replacing them with pizza night. Now I *know* that would enlighten my life.

———

Did you ever get into that argument with the voice in your head?

He says: "Let's go brush our teeth before bed."

And I don't want to even though I ate a truckload of Doritos and then sodomized the refrigerator. Sometimes, I just hate that voice. I would just like to kick its ass. But who would I brag to about it? You tell that cute tale to anyone and you can end up a mandatory guest at Club Wackadoo.

I know I've been asking a lot of questions about pot tonight and I'm sorry, but I do have a sound reason for that. You see, each show I do I set a goal. I try to get at least one pot virgin to give it a try. It's not addictive and it's a lot of fun. Sure, you may giggle uncontrollably, but only because you feel so good. And ladies, I have but two words for you:

Aphro. Disiac

Chapter 2:
Social Disasters in My Little World

I only screw with people who deserve to be screwed with.

Example: A good friend of mine is about 175 pounds overweight. He was always a fat bastard. When he was born, he put his mom in a wheelchair.

For 20 years, I nicely told him he had to lose weight. He finally listened to me the one time I yelled at him, but I yelled at him for a good reason. Wednesday, I have this thing with the pizza dude. At 6:00 every Wednesday night, I have a large sausage pizza delivered and I leave this kid a six-pack in my mailbox. It's completely win/win. And if I don't answer the door, he leaves it on the picnic table.

One night I come home and there's this fat bastard picking his teeth with the last of *my* fucking crust. So I said, "The hell is wrong with you?" Know what his excuse was? The pizza man handed it to him.

So again, I said, "You fat bastard, get the hell out of my yard." I may have said, 'Get the fuck out of my yard,' but I'm trying to curb the use of that word a bit. If a sentence needs to be enhanced by it however, I won't fail to whip it out…

The F bomb, if you were thinking something else, because my 'whippin it out' days are over.

He called me up a week later and apologized. Then he said he was losing weight and invited me over.

And, no, I did not forget about my freakin pizza. He is gonna pay. I will bust his will. Before I went over, I sucked down a big ol stinky Italian hoagie with triple servings of the raw onions. Then I picked up a case of beer.

I knock on his front door and breathe really fast till he opens the door so there's a hoagie cloud to greet him. That caught him off guard. The rest of the night I couldn't help but feel that anytime I exhaled, he would inhale; like he was feasting on my breath. He got to a point where he'd lean in to talk to me and I'd have to cut a fart to move him back a little.

"Breathe deep on that you pizza gobbling bastard!" Then I started drinking beer in front of him. After I finished a six-pack, he asked for one. I said, "The beer bone is connected to the pizza bone."

He understood and agreed. So I drank every beer in front of him. Even with a nice buzz like that, I knew he was weakening. So I crashed on his sofa and he went to bed. At 4:00 a.m. I woke up hungry; so I got some cloves of garlic and butter and cooked it down. Then I spread it over a baguette. It smelled wonderful and tasted even better.

His bedroom door pops open and he fires a shot over my head; he told me to drop the roll and get the hell out... Oh yeah, I broke him.

Now I have to find a new football buddy. Do you know how hard it is to find someone my age who can relax in a bar and drink more than two beers because 'his wild drinking days are over'? Believe it or not, these dudes are freakin everywhere.

My god, fellas relax. That's why they invented the fuckin taxi. Older people are afraid of fun. Going to the bar is like a relatively cheap mini vacation; and if you wake up tomorrow…YAY!

That's the thrill of it. Get out of the house. Get the stink blown off. To tell the truth, sports are okay too. They help with this.

———

I'm a sports fan…to a point. I don't cry and stomp my feet if my team loses. That's life, grow the fuck up. I see this crap when I go over to my friend's house. I've gone over to peoples' houses 2 weeks after the Super Bowl and still felt the tension. I asked one dude why he was so down. He said; "The refs gave the Super Bowl away."

INSTANTANEOUSLY I bitch-slapped him. "It's just a game dude."

Apparently he never thought of that, and life again became good. I love watching soccer fans kill each other, don't you? I didn't pay 20 quid to watch my teams arse get kicked from pole to bloody pole. Someone has got to die!

You just don't get that kind of passion and anger from synchronized swimming. Everyone gets a nice round of applause before heading to the beer concession. It's just a game played by people far more superior in athletics than you. You're not a better person if your team wins. If your team finally wins after 25 years and it's the best moment of your life, well…Sir, have had a pretty sad life.

If I was to compare the emotions these sports nuts feel, I'd have to say they're close to gambling. If I crap out at craps or 22 my 21, I get upset. I do not like to gamble and lose. If

I'm laying my mortgage down on a hard 10, I want that son-of-a-bitch to come up. I've seen people punch their TV's. I have punched slot machines. But your TV punchers aren't breaking the law. Apparently, I am.

I've heard every line that could come out of a security guard's mouth. "Stop punching the machines, sir. Stop biting the machines, sir. Stop crowbarring the machines sir." I've developed a universal theory that time travel is impossible, using the common gambler as my side board. If a gambler looses a thousand dollars and is poor, he can go back in time to when he first got there and go back to the slot machine next to the one he lost at, and just keep on going till it hits.

I guess it's obvious to you folks that a thought like that only comes after a night of bad gambling.

But I do like those casinos...especially in Phila.

———

Yes, it happened again. A casino in Phila has yet again had to have someone arrested for leaving their kid locked in a car while they were inside gambling.

How much of an ass are *you* going to look like when the dust settles? It can get pretty bad.

Prosecutor: "Mr. Sir, what was the conversation you had with your child before you locked him in the car with the windows shut?"

Scumbag: "I uh, well, I says to him, come on Jimmy, I think they have an arcade here. And he said, "No, that's okay Dad. I wanna finish reading this book.""

Prosecutor: "Wrong Sir, wrong. We have witnesses that saw you giving him Ny-Quil so he'd sleep."

Scumbag: "No…no…he had that…what's that thing called? A sneeze? No, uh…that hacking thing, you know…a cough? That's what he had. He had a cough."

Prosecutor: "Wrong again. The witnesses say you bragged about it while walking to the casino."

Scumbag: "I left him a balloon so he'd have someone to talk to."

Prosecutor: "You're right. You are 'father of the year'; we may just let you go… Oh, wait, wait…let's just make sure of all the facts here, Sir. It says you were arrested on March 1st. Well look at that, you were arrested on your son's birthday… His *second* birthday."

Scumbag: "That explains the balloon."

Prosecutor: "Your Honor: Permission to beat the prisoner within an inch of his life?"

Judge: "Permission granted."

We need corporal punishment to come
back. Crack a couple skulls, smash some hands.
I think the crime rate would drop a lot. Prison
isn't a deterrent unless some big guy 'buddy's
up' to your tail pipe. *Then* you'll wish you
payed those parking tickets.

If I ever did find myself in that exact scenario, I would use every lie I could think of to stall for time.

"Uh, I have bad diarrhea. You don't want that on your...bat."

"Do they have an AIDS support group in here?"

"My Daddy is rich and I'll give you a million dollars if you don't bang me."

I like to think of myself as a problem solver. You know, giving answers to unasked problems.

———

Not only do I try to give earth shattering solutions to some of the world's biggest problems, but I also tackle some of the smaller ones. And some stuff that's just flat-out stupid.

Like, if you have a pot brownie and you get the munchies so you have another brownie and you get the munchies again so you have another brownie, will you eventually die from this? Or do you pass out with a huge ring of chocolate around your mouth? Or is this where fat people come from? F.Y.I: This scenario can be used for lots of things besides brownies.

I saw a girl put the better part of a kettle full of spaghetti down her throat. And I stood there laughing to myself, "She really thinks its oregano." I amused myself as I counted how many times she refilled her plate…7…7 plates. I watched her go up 2 dress sizes right there.

There's something so unsexy about a girl with more than half her face covered in spaghetti sauce. And nobody told her. Hey, the bitch drank my last beer! I needed this. Before someone eventually told her, we got our picture taken together. I have a smile on my face so big I look like I'm about to burst. Why? Because…DON'T DRINK MY LAST BEER.

We all do dumb things. My last dumb thing was a couple of days ago. I let one of my sons borrow my car and, as he's driving away, I realize my phone is in the car. Well he doesn't see me waving my hands like some retard on fire. So I start feeling around in my pockets, looking for my phone so I can call him to have him spin back around and give me my phone. That went on for about 5 seconds. Okay, let's let some of the slower people catch up. *(Pause and Hum)*

Don't you find it exciting when you see someone about to do something stupid and you don't say a word? You just wait to see if it happens. I was at a barbeque one time and this one dude just kept walking through the sliding kitchen door: Inside outside inside outside.

Well, the door was open all day but it started getting chilly so I closed it. Did I mention it was a clear glass door? So he's getting ready to come in…again, and I'm watching him and he's kinda waving to me. I'm pretty sure he didn't realize the door was closed.

I've replayed this in my mind 10,000 times: Slow motion, fast motion, normal speed. And I let him walk face-first into the door. I mean, the shocked look on his face was priceless. I couldn't stop laughing. He broke his big toe and kind of mashed his nose. It made it all the funnier. Of course, he doesn't invite me over anymore. Hey, I had too many friends anyway. I'll occasionally trade a mediocre friendship for a hilarious lifetime memory.

That one was relatively easy to make a decision about whether or not to warn him. At the crucial time, my brain finally said, "Fuck him." So we sat there and watched...*Splat*.

With another friend, I saw a potential for real danger. I went to his house and he was getting ready to go up his step ladder. It's at the top of the steps and only 3 legs of the ladder were on solid ground; the fourth step was hanging out over the top step into space.

As he was walking toward the ladder, I thought to myself, "This is gonna hurt and I can stop it if I want to." So I did. I told him it was unsafe...or at least that's what I told my mom. Yeah, the ol brain said, "Fuck him too." But at least now I'm at a level number of friends I can balance.

As he was falling, he was grasping at anything with both hands that he could find to stop himself from falling; unfortunately, the only thing there was a whole lot of air. I thought about trying to grab his arm, but the way he was falling around he'd have taken me with him. And somebody has to call the ambulance. I can't do that with a cracked skull. I think 'brain' and I came to the same conclusion at the same time, "bad idea" and "fuck him."

And if we're still talking about stupid things that people do, my neighbor, Bob, let me listen in on one of his conversations with his daughter. I was telling him how easy a job it was to raise two sons as opposed to him raising one daughter. As he's telling me this, his phone rang and it was his daughter. He says, "Okay, listen to this." Then he put his phone on speaker:

Daughter: "Daddy, is that you?"

Bob: "Yes Pumpkin, what's up?"

Daughter: "Daddy, I just hit another car."

Bob: "Geez, are you okay? Did you call a cop?"

Daughter: "Oh, I'm fine daddy, the guy I hit is kinda limping around and, as luck would have it, he's a cop."

Bob: "Did he say anything to you?"

Daughter: "Besides 'what the hell is the matter with you?' No, but he did call his lawyer and then an ambulance."

Bob: "My god, how did this happen?"

Daughter: "Well, when I saw him, I panicked and did the opposite of what you're supposed to do."

Bob: "You hit the gas instead of the brake?"

Daughter: "No, I turned toward him instead of away from him."

It was at about this time I pointed to the door and whispered, "I'll just let myself out."

———

I think the stupidest people are the ones that think they're smart. And before you start overanalyzing that statement, let me dumb it down. I mean, explain it to you.

There are people out there who love to try and finish your sentences as you're talking to them. I'm not talking about married couples. As an observer of their type of behavior, I must tell you it's cute but we, the observers, find it disturbing. We know it's the final thread that's holding the tapestry of your marriage together.

And once that's gone, you may want to start cooking your own meals. You'd be amazed how much radiator fluid you can put into your mate's chicken noodle soup before they notice a change in flavor. But...I digress.

So I'm at a party and I'm telling stories about the movie I made last year. There was about six people...or five, and one jackass listening to me. And as I'm finishing each sentence, this guy would throw out the last word.

Me: "So that's how I met Hugh."

Jackass: "Jackman."

Me: "He was really—"

Jackass: "Cool."

I had to get rid of this slug so I switched gears.

Me: "Actually, it was kind of boring out there. Some days I would lock my dressing room door and play with my—"

Jackass: "Pinga."

Me: "Well, I was gonna say 'small train set I brought from home', but if you wanna picture me fiddling my faddle who am I to stop you from picturing me spiddling on your noggin?"

Job done. Jackass magically disappeared.

———

I'd like to start doing more TV pretty soon. It's so boring now and I think I could really spice it up. The last surprise I got from the TV was the O.J. trial. I just kind of blinked my eyes and said, "HAHAHAA… really?"

Did you ever walk by your TV and hear a commercial that stops you in your tracks? No? Me neither. It would really have to be so outrageous that I'd HAVE to listen to it.

You want an example? Okay, here's one I'd have to listen to.

"Hey Rockers, it's the motor city madman, Ted Nugent, here with a word about Cialis."

That would plant my feet. That would leave skid marks behind me. My brain would just fill with a pool of strange questions.

"Did you lose a bet? Do you owe the IRS? Did you try to use your pinga for an arrow? What happened, Ted?"

Then he breaks into the Ted Nugent we all know and love.

"I'm banging my granddaughter's friends so my pinga is just fine. But guys, I know some of you are shooting bear with blanks. You can't fake a stiff pinga. When you can't do the job, they come to me.

It was fine 40 years ago and the ink on their high school diplomas was still wet, but a lot of your women are really grossing me out. Have you ever considered showing your wives what a salad looks like? Fella, I understand the paradox. You want to make love to a woman, just not *your* woman. I get it. I don't want them either so just take the damn pill!

Thank you, Mr. Nugent."

———

How much garbage must be in your house to be considered a hoarder? I've been in a lot of people's houses and have seen some weird things.

One dude I knew had a weird thing for pizza boxes…would you call that a fetish? And I admit it, your average pizza box is very cool, but after 12 hours, out it must go. After 12 hours, it's a stinking empty box.

This dude had hundreds all around his condo. To be fair, some were probably mine. I'd have pizza parties and when they were over, he'd volunteer to put them in my recycling bucket. Next day, there were no pizza boxes out there. I feel funny, like I was robbed, you know? I just couldn't bring myself to tell him to give me my garbage back. I'd kinda sound like an ass.

He used to play this game where you'd put a blindfold on him and hand him any box. He could tell you what joint it came from and what was on it. Or at least I think that's what he did. Actually, when he put on the blindfold, we handed him the box, grabbed all the beer and quietly left out the back door.

We did leave him a note in the fridge where the beer used to be: "Get laid, dude."

Except for his pizza box harem he was a normal guy; never late for work, lots of friends, blackout drunk every Friday night...you know a normal fella.

He was the guy that told me a friend of a friend of a cousin's friend told somebody that he had a swollen colon. So his, you know…poop…was a little thicker than dental floss. He once claimed fame for producing a 50-foot turd; he said it looked like a plate of brown linguini.

Now this is why I keep a tight inner circle. There is too much of that going on that I don't want to know about. The dark is good. It's colon-story-free.

Speaking of people not in my circle…

———

Divorce is not something to be made fun of…no, I'm kidding, of course it is. Like, if you're the one that got hurt, be the one that decides where negotiations take place. And obviously, before lawyers get involved.

If I may, I'd like to suggest a few places that might help speed these negotiations up a bit. How about next to a shark tank? Your former better half may accidentally slip and…chomp chomp chomp.

If you don't like fish, a firing range will do. Let him or her fire a shot then put a slug in their

temple. Then switch guns with them. They'll
have gunpowder residue on their hands and the
bullet will match the gun. See, I learned a lot
from years of 'C.S.I.' viewing.

I think I'd be really careful if I screwed my
wife over. Eat only wrapped foods and drink
beer in a can. Check my brakes every day.
Never know. Oh, and dull up the steak knives.

Not everyone divorces though. Eskimos
have a low divorce rate. Probably because
they've become frozen together.

You gotta give it to the Eskimos. A
summer day up North is like 2 degrees. Yet
every 20 years there's another generation of
Eskimos. I can't even pee outside if it's under
40. And sex would be awkward...unfulfilling,
seeing as that I'd be looking for wood to burn.

I was just watching a documentary on them
and, not to sound ignorant, but a lot of them
look alike. I'll bet it's like just a couple guys in
electric underwear knocking up the women.
While all the men are out of the village making

whale jerky, these dudes roll in and bang all the women…it's obvious.

And it's probably a couple Italian guys. They're pretty warm-blooded, right? Ask any Italian guy that ever had sex and he'll tell you he can bang a snow-woman so hard that by the time he's done, he's jacking off into a snowball.

I'm sorry. I don't like doing ethnic humor. You never know, some folks can't take a joke. One of these guidos might shove a derringer in my ear, *capiece*?

I'm not Eskimo or Italian, but I'm part German. I have guilt though about what some of my people have done. No, not "allegedly" done, these freaking people did it. Every once in a while they like to fuck up the world a little bit. It takes about 3 generations to forgive them and then they fuck it up again.

There are times where I thought I could cleanse the German part of my soul, such as stopping stupid shit like saying, auf Wiedersehen to my hand and putting it in a blender. Then a little Gestapo voice whispers in my brain, "Dumkoff, fuck that."

I don't usually bombard a story with so many F bombs, but with Germans you kind of have to.

I'm also part Irish. I believe I'm a fifth… uh. Huh…come on now, one of my kids wrote that. It's cute.

And I know it's fashionable to talk about the wild drinking of the Irish, like "Bobbing for stones in a keg of Jameson whiskey;" or the leprechaun hunt after Chugapalooza.

No, I'm not going to "exploit" these ridiculous stereotypes. I want to talk about Irish women. I love them.

A beautiful drunken Irish woman of questionable moral standards will give you a night you'll never forget. My little "O Johnson" stands at attention whenever I think of those nights.

I think the Irish are really on to something. They go to work, come home and get drunk.

And, if you think about it, being a cop a hundred years ago would have been the perfect job for an Irishman. Back then you could take your frustrations out on the criminals you caught; a hard knee here, a nightstick there. Of course they were frustrated back then. If there were no criminals, they wouldn't have a job. Then they'd be home drinking and banging their wives. I'd be busting heads too.

You see, when Irish couples meet, when they're dating, sex is for the love of each other. When they get married they take out life insurance policies on each other. After a while, when they grow tired of looking at each other, they try to kill each other. And the best way to do it is "heart attack in the sack." Try and knock out their whiskey-soaked ticker.

After 5 years of the best "bump and grind" you've ever had, you realize that's the best sex you'll ever get. Then you spend the next 45 years listening to each other's bad accent…very sad…and that's all true…

I have a little piece of French in me too, but don't hold it against me. I'm a nice guy. Does anybody know why the French look down on us? Didn't we save their ass in WWII?

I was in a French restaurant one time and my waiter was talking down to me. I didn't know what he said but I didn't like how he was saying it.

I got bugged by this guy. Finally I said, "Dude, I will bitch slap that fucked up accent off your frog lips if you don't change your attitude."

Of course, I didn't eat my food when it came out...I could see this d-bag sticking his snail into my bouillabaisse.

They think *we're* dirty people yet their women roll their underarm hair in curlers. To hell with that, I'm going back to Ireland.

Chapter 3:
Crazy Bitches & the Guys Who Love Them

Guys, I'm gonna let the ladies in on a little secret about us. Now don't worry, I think some of the ladies may already suspect it. I don't think it's gonna be a big shock.

Okay ladies, occasionally...men *do* lie. Not even a gasp, huh?

Okay, now, see that guys? Too many of you are telling bad lies. Either start telling better lies or stop lying.

A bad lie might sound like this: A newlywed couple live three days in their honeymoon suite. They don't leave the room. They're trying to wear out each other's genitalia. And nobody comes in. They sustain each other on bodily fluids...yummy.

She goes to the bathroom, comes out and asks if you left the toilet seat up.

Guys, don't say no. She freakin knows you did. She didn't leave it up so take the freakin heat on this one. You're making us all look bad.

Guys, when you lie she cannot know it. That's the point of lying...to get out of trouble. Some lies are more like loopholes.

Here's an example: A husband and wife are taking a long ride. He knows it's a long ride but she doesn't. After driving for three hours she asks you if, "you're almost there."

You can say, yeah, even though you know it's still 2 hours away. If she mentions it when you get there, just head to the bar. If she mentions it while you're still driving, slip some NyQuil into her Diet Dr. Pepper. That will get her to shut the hell up.

Lying to women is so easy, but your lie has to be about something they'd never expect.

Guys...how many of you have faked an orgasm? You're just not in the mood or you're tired. So you let them ride you like a jockey till they get their jolly...or jolly's, then you let out a couple moans, roll over, and say goodnight. The lie doesn't really matter at this point. She doesn't care.

I faked an orgasm last week. I was great…fine acting. I just didn't want sex right then. I had it a few hours before with someone else and I just couldn't "cross the finish line." This particular day, the lies just started to rack up fast.

She asked if she was the only one and I said, "Yes." I didn't go into detail that she was the only one…that afternoon.

And when she asked if I had a test to check for sexual diseases, I said, "Yes. In April." I didn't go into details like, "April 1983."

See how fast they add up? It's like juggling answers. A couple more lies and you can really get into trouble. She may pull a pop quiz later that night, and you have to keep the "facts" straight.

You do not want to be caught in that web. If you don't give the answer with the same enthusiasm that you gave when you were weaving this tapestry of bullshit, the little bullshit detector she has in her brain will go off and then she wants more details about something you said that you forgot as you were saying it.

That sound that follows is the vacuum of existence. In layman's terms, you're listening to your house of fucking cards crashing down all around you.

You don't want to be there for that.

The minute you sense the playback beginning, get yourself out of there. Make dinner reservations, go to work, just leave. Walk out of the house and say nothing.

Now you have a couple hours to come up with another stinking pile of, uh, imaginative storytelling. Here's an example:

Her: "Where did you go? Why did you just walk out like that?"

You: "I thought I was having a stroke and I didn't want to worry you so I just left without saying a thing. Then I walked to the hospital."

Her: "The hospital? Well what did they say?"

You: "Well, actually…"

(Note: Try not to say 'actually.' We think that word sets off the bullshit detectors.)

Okay, let's see how deep he can dig his hole and still crawl out…

You: "Well, actually…by the time I got there it started to clear up. Five minutes later, I felt great."

She: "But you were gone for 6 hours."

You: "Well then I went out for a couple beers to celebrate being stroke-free."

She: "How many beers?"

Okay, now do you see how she's vacuuming up finer details of the story? She picked up on something and we, the guys from the A.R.I. (Alternate Reality Inc.), believe it was when you said, 'actually.' We're still running tests.

Now you have to pay extra attention to your answers. Try to associate your answers to things in your life you won't forget. If your lucky number is 3, then you had 3 beers even if you had 20. Now that kind of lie is like the mortar that's gonna hold the new house of bullshit together. It's kind of important you remember that.

Another thing to remember, the playback might not start for 5 days while she sucks up every detail she needs. Stay calm. Don't go storing your answers too deeply just yet. It could start in 5 seconds too. Don't trip over your own feet.

We also believe the 5 second playback is directly linked to the woman's pre-menstrual syndrome. They seem a bit more bloodthirsty then…uh, sorry about that. Now watch out for landmines…

Her: "So you had 3 beers?"

You: "Yup…3."

Her: "Female bartender?" *landmine.*

You: "Uh, no…some short guy." *More mortar.*

She: "How many beers?"

You: "Seventeen…uh, 3.

See how she probably picked up on that right away? You may want to pull another Houdini. If I lie to women for sex and not money, does that still make me a bad person? Yeah, I pulled the old, "It's My Birthday" gag when it wasn't really my birthday.

You know, like the second date and you're trying to speed up the process…you know…have sex? And in the first 5 minutes of the second date you're sensing it isn't going to happen tonight because she's acting reserved. So when she asks what you want to do tonight, say, "Well, it's my 45th birthday today. *(45 is more bullshit.)*

And she'll be like, "OMG, I didn't know that. We have to get a drink…"

Me: "Okay, honey. I was thinking the same thing."

After 5 or 6 pitchers of Long Island Iced Tea I'm usually being dragged by my little love handles into the bedroom. And usually everything is on the table. Inhibitions were drowned by the third pitcher.

And if you know anything about me, you know I am not shy.

There was a concern I had as I was creating this ploy. And no, not 'what if she wanted to look at my license?' I'd just shove a bottle of rum down her throat so far that she wouldn't remember what she asked.

My big fear was 'what if I do a farm animal freak fest with a chick and fall in love with her?' I mean, chains drag me to the altar for my castration…I'm ready.

Chapter 4:
Sex Part III: When Appendages Attack

As I hit the half-century mark, my goals changed from when I was 25.

First, I still want to go to Yosemite Park. That goal has not changed. I just haven't found the time.

Second, I want to have sex with a woman half my age. Obviously, this was not my past goal. I think at 25 I banged a 50-year-old lady. And it was good. I remember the stupid ass line that I used on this lady at a bar. "How would you like me to knock you out of the ballpark?" She practically carried me to her room. I just might have been *her* goal.

Does it bother any of you if I talk about casual sex? And I mean *so* casual you hardly knew you had it. And age differences. When is it considered…disgusting?

I thought the 'Anna Nicole Smith and Marshall the Billionaire' was a pretty disgusting mental picture. I don't blame him. No, no, and *bravo* on your choice, dead guy. If I ever wake up one day and I'm a billionaire I'm gonna find me a dingy blonde, brick house…but only a redhead.

I guess she just laid back and clicked the meter on. Every stroke was money, ten million and one dollar, ten million and two dollars, ten million and…she got like 400 million dollars and, in my opinion, earned it.

How could she smile having this wrinkly, old motherfucker crawling all over her body? YUCK! Coke, lots of coke. She was probably amazed every time he didn't die after crawling off her, or calling in the nurse to help him up off her.

Hey, do old people think about that? Like, your mate could die of an orgasm induced heart attack? And you have to sit there and explain what happened. What about if you didn't quite reach the finish line? Sad way to go out...

That would be a great way of sending someone off...by finishing yourself off.

Am I offending anybody talking about sex with the dead? No...alright, good. Because I've been wanting to talk about sex in a morgue. Do you think that happens? Some gorgeous body comes in after overdosing. Do you think it happens...like, a lot? I've seen some of these guys and some of them have a look in their eyes like they've fucked the dead.

And I'm sure a few female morticians have ridden their share of rigormortis pingas.

I couldn't do it. I just couldn't. I'm sorry if I'm disappointing you. I may be able to get over the whole dead thing but...it's cold. Yuck.

Why do guys like to stick that thing everywhere? I read a story about a guy who fucked a live beehive. I don't get it. And I'm not that kind of guy. I'm sorry, I'm not that freaky with my crank. Not to mention, bees are mean.

Give me 2 or 3 girls at once and my 47 positions and I'm done. I guess I'm kind of a prude.

Wait, wasn't I talking about goals about an hour ago? I have one more goal. I want a strain of marijuana named after me. Buffalo Morgan Gold. I like that. And if they could sell it in bags that have a picture of me giving the thumbs-up sign, *then* I would have left behind the ultimate legacy.

———

It gets harder, the older I get.

I'm talking about dating! Let's try it again from another angle. Dating women in their 30's and 40's has its downsides. A lot of women are having body pains or are on medications for something or other. If they're on the fence about if we're having sex or not, a couple drinks used to tilt the scale in my favor. Not now. They're worried about side effects. Alcohol was my Plan B. but some can't lay on their backs.

Some can't lay on their fronts. How do you sleep?

I met a woman who'd just had her scootch overhauled. She said she couldn't 'bang bang' for 6 weeks. So I looked her in the eyes and said, "Okay, but what did your dentist say?"

Thank you…I love that joke, too. It's not mine but I love it.

———

I look at women as works of art…of course there are a couple Picassos in there. You're pretty sure it's a chick because it's wearing flannel. And no, I don't sleep with every woman that asks me for casual sex. I've turned down free scootch…twice. Well, once. The other time I was in a coma. My pinga wasn't in a coma. He wanted to in the worst way when the offer was made. He was practically barking at the nurse. All of a sudden, the bitch got a case of the scruples. She did give him a nice long kiss. That was kind of her. I know he liked that.

I'll bet you're wondering how I could possibly know this if I was in a coma. Well, to be honest with you I wasn't really in a coma. I faked it. I faked a coma…you know, I was burned out. I faked a coma just to get off the road. The puppeteers that control me are a couple of greedy bastards.

And that's how they sign my checks: "Please make checks payable to: *Show Pony*, in the amount of Dink-Denk-Squeak such and such dollars. Signed: *Greedy Bastards, Inc.*

Know what? I'd like to get a psychological profile of any woman who would give head to a guy allegedly in a coma. My ego would love to believe she's a fan. But what if she does this to every guy who's in a coma? Now *that,* Paris Hilton, is hot.

The other woman I turned down I'm not even 100% sure she was a woman. I'm not even sure it was even human. It was big, hairy and horrible…and I was scared. I had a couple drinks with it hoping she would pass out. She wouldn't even go to the bathroom so I could run out, like a weasel.

Finally, she got her nerve up to say, "How would you like to take me upstairs and—"

"No," I said before she finished.

So she tilted her head in amazement. "I was going to ask if you wanted to fuck me."

"Oh, I know what you were asking me. And no, I don't want to fuck you."

Even if I had a dozen orgasms, I couldn't see me walking out her door *not* hating myself.

And what if I get selective E.D.? It can happen. I could look down and he could be like, "Are you *out* of your mind? Look at that! I'm not doing that. I'm going over here and reading a book. Tell her I'm on strike. Give her the old, 'This never happened before' line. And for god's sake tell her to put her shirt back on, she's wilting the flowers and they're not even *real*."

So after I said no she really got defensive. It was like I was the first guy to turn her down. I couldn't imagine any guy going for it...*unless* he was in a coma. There you go.

———

The cute nurse should be out at the bar banging a different guy every night and Princess Heffer should be riding coma guys. Bet if anyone *was* faking a coma, they'd have a miraculous recovery when they saw what was heading their way.

So, know what she said to me? She said, "Why not? Are you a homo?"

I was shocked, but not shocked enough to say, "No, I'm just not into bestiality."

She tried to pour her drink on my head but, out of reflex, I looked up, opened my mouth, and caught every drop. I don't know what she was drinking but it was pretty good.

Okay, I admit it. I'm a junkie. When a woman offers me free sex I have to take it. It's like my creed. I think the world would be a better place if you just go up to complete strangers and ask them for sex. And they either say yes or no…no questions asked.

So you see, I can't turn it away. What kind of example would I be setting?

It's alright for women to get away with that type of behavior. I will say nothing against that type of woman. But if a guy does that, he's either drunk or gets high on mace.

I'd like to think if I had enough money I could have any woman just once. I hope before I go senile. It's a real movie in my head that, when I'm old, I'll walk up to women half a century younger than me and ask them, "How many hundreds do I have to peel off the wad to get them panties off?

Wait a minute…what? Why didn't I bang the nurse if she was cute? Dude that was a half hour ago. We covered a lot of ground since then…okay, I'll tell you. If I blew my coma cover, my agent would book me somewhere that night and trot me out on stage. I know. I faked 3 comas and always blew it with a horny nurse.

An hour later, I'm on a plane heading for Moose Scrotum, Ontario.

You know, I'm pretty lucky when it comes to finding horny nurses. I'll bet they're not even nurses at all. I'm thinking my agent hires a hooker to dress as a nurse to try to wake me by any means possible.

Geez, maybe I *did* eat too much acid as a kid.

———

It must be terrible to lust over a woman you can never have. In the nineties there were a lot of crappy movies made to show a man's softer side. How gay…no offense.

And all it showed was 'if you're annoying and persistent, you can have anybody on the planet.' When I say I have her, I don't mean 'wearing a third sock, hiding in the closet' have her.

I mean, "And this is my room; my, aren't they lovely. Bang, bang, boing, boing, gush, gush, flesh and blood woman."

I think I'm in need of a great sex vacation. No rollercoasters, no freaking oceans, no people. Well, maybe just one, and a couple gallons of rum. It should also have a great view so when you're getting reloaded after round one, you got something else beautiful to look at.

The only awkward thing for men on a sex vacation is the time between round one and round two. After you both catch your breath, the woman is usually ready to go while we have to wait for the return of "The Great Actor." And if you have to take a little blue pill to give Chester a little kick in the ass back on the stage…so be it.

By round 5, your fantasy paradise of a Utopian lust fest has degenerated into bad food, warm liquor, and the senseless slapping of 2 exhausted carcasses. And if you did it right, most of day 2 will be spent letting the wounds heal a bit. No matter how much lube you burned through, you should still have friction burns.

That's why rum is my choice of band aid. It reminds me that I can heal after the vacation is over and it's time to make some fresh wounds.

When you can't afford to do something with your mate, sex is cheap enough. And the rhyme method flies right out the window after a couple cheap beers.

You have to innovate when you're poor. If you can't afford to pick up condoms on the way home, a Snickers wrapper will do in a pinch.

I believe the poor think about sex a lot more than rich people do. A rich guy would probably say, "What a beautiful day for a ride on the yacht." And the poor guy is like, "I may not know what a yacht is…or how to spell it, but I can sure spell scootch and I'd rather ride that.

Let me know if I get a little close to the line, will ya please?

Have you ever made love in a limo before? I did…it wasn't my limo either. It was parked at a Stuckey's and the driver was just leaving. Once inside, we knocked on the door of it. No one answered so we went in; we weren't neat about it either. Once we got into a good rhyme with the shock absorbers, it was all over. I could see why rich folk love doing it in there. I hope the owner looked before he sat down. That'd be a nasty way to know your car has been violated.

———

I have gotten hurt during sex but I still had to act manly. Yeah baby, come on baby, yeah, I'll make you see the future. But inside I was saying, "It hurts, it hurts, it hurts."

And when we were done and I got up to go to the bathroom, she said, "Why are you walking like your balls are on fire?"

I said, "If my balls were on fire I'd be running and, secondly, shut the fuck up."

Yeah, I was hurting. I think I pulled a nut...and not in a good way.

Now that's giving 110%. You bring pleasure to another person while you block your own pain; that's a hero in my book. The stuff of legend.

Get a folk song written about me. Find Pete Seeger. That M.F.er's still alive, isn't he?

When you have sex for the first time, you know you were bad. It's not even a question. You tried, but you were so happy to get there, you just poked around for 3 seconds then, *splat*.

The second time you have a little more confidence. You may even make it all the way in before, *splat*. If you're a girl that never did it with a guy that never did it, you may worry that that's as good as it gets. Trust me darlings, it gets better.

There's a real problem with people who are…let's say, 'sexually casual.'

You meet someone on the street who you've recently had a one night stand with. Depending on how it ended will decide how the conversation will go. See if you can figure out who just wanted a nice night and who just got their heart broken:

NUMBER 1:

He: "Brenda? Hi honey. How've you been?"

She: "John, so good to see you."

Oohh... if only the world was like that. Now, see if this sounds familiar.

NUMBER 2:

He: "Oh, hi...Peg...Peggy. How are you doing?"

She: "You bastard. You gave me crabs."

He: "Yeah, I meant to call you about that but, by day 3, I figured you knew."

She: "FUCK YOU."

He: "I'll see you around."

You see now, dude? Number 2 has virtually no chance of a repeat performance. While number 1 can probably get another shot if he puts it out there.

If you wanna be a player live by these 2 rules: Don't give somebody something you don't want given to you. No S.T.D.'s and no little creepy crawlies, crabs, lobsters...whatever.

Rule 2: Don't be *too* good in bed. Save the fancy stuff for when you're in love. If you're a sexual athlete, you don't have to prove it to everyone you boink. Eventually, someone may not want you to leave.

Then the "L" word gets slung around and it can really get messy once your folks sober up. It's usually about this time one of you goes into the bathroom to clean your pinga while your mate slips out the hotel door…YOU WHORE! Sorry about that. I'm beginning to make progress with my therapy.

———

Speaking of reading…

I read in some rag that a 75-year-old virgin just got married. The groom says he can't wait. So I say to you, Mr. Groom…you *can* wait.

Of all the ways my brain chooses to look at this story, there just are no bright cheery pictures of this. It can go from her "chickening out" to his, "I think I broke my hip." Or any of a dozen other disasters that I can pull from the sky.

Hey buddy, you probably had better times in your life…a lot of better times. But don't get yourself too worked up there, pops. You might get halfway in when your heart explodes. Remember, if you die on top of her, that might be great for you but, guaranteed, she won't bang anybody ever again.

Even if she forgets the emotional trauma, her scootch is one for one. She hit a grand slam her first time at bat. Nobody ever does that. She'd have to retire after batting a thousand.

But isn't that everyone's goal? To try and drive your mate into the next world…why are you guys looking at me like that? Does nobody in the room know how to fuck?

Hey, I'm nice and gentle and all that other crap, but she's gonna know I was there. If you're not going to show her how much you appreciate her banging you, why bother?

And if she's your wife, you should *really*
give it to her. Need motivation? Easy: If you
don't wanna bang her, you have a dozen friends
who would.

"You whore."

Sorry. That was a friend of mine from
therapy. This guy has
fetishes…real…sick…fetishes. I'm only there to
get fresh material. I'm okay. Really.

———

So this guy has a foot fetish for one. And I
made the mistake of showing up in sandals.
Every time I looked his way, I'd catch him
smiling at my feet before looking away.

Finally I said, "Dude, if you're of a mind to
fuck my toes, I have a pretty wicked backhand
that might do you some good."

Sorry folks, but that kind of stuff creeps me
out. Your feet walk on all the dirt imbedded in
carpets, all the dirt on hardwood floors, and all
the dirt in dirt. Why would anyone want to suck

on your toes, or whatever it is you do…?

YUCK!

He has a hair fetish. He loves eating women's hair. He's admitted in group therapy that he gets off nibbling on his wife's hair while she sleeps. That is just fuckin creepy.

If I was asleep and whoever I slept with that night was nibbling my hair, and I woke up, I'd be freaked out. And I think the hotter the woman was, the more freaked I'd be. So far I've only been woken up by pleasant surprises. I like being woken up as a meal or a pony.

You'll get it later.

See, I told you. Group therapy is great for new material. It's because of you folks that I search out only the finest sexual misconduct this world has to offer. If we don't know that these sexual weirdos exist, how can we ever join them?

And…if you're not a freak, you're not an asshole. You're unique, like a Siamese twin.

Speaking of which, if you're banging a Siamese twin what's the other chick doing? I could see the fun of the other one jumping in but I doubt it'd happen. Probably just watch…and that's unacceptable. Even if she jumps in, I don't think it technically counts as a ménage a trois. But it could count as a threesome. Man, sex can be so complicated.

And that's why some people with 12 kids had so many kids, because they can't understand the basic principle of how babies are made. "If I put this thing in, that is what comes out. *(Since you can't see me, I point to pinga for in and point to daughter for out.)*

That might have been a heavy thought to follow. I can get pretty deep…it's deep for me.

———

I know every woman has either fantasized or *had* an anaconda man. You know, a guy over a foot long? You know…here…

How about that first moment you realize he is not like other men. Like on that first date, you're both drinking in a bar and she slaps your knee and says, "Oh my god, you're so funny... What the fuck is this?" Unless you're a total derelict, you should be able to close the deal from here.

From then on, that is your leash. She will pull you home.

I had the exact opposite happen to me...*let's forget I said that and I'll try again.*

Most men have fantasies that the woman they are about to make love to for the first time is like banging a Froot Loop. And I don't mean some crazy bitch that likes doing wild sexual stuff with concrete. I mean a low mileage Kung-Fu grip scootch. Now *that* is an overrated male fantasy.

4

Get it off your bucket list because it does
not end well. I have a story that starts happy but
ends badly.

You're gonna hear this because, you know,
it's what I do.

Okay, I'm secretly in love with this girl for
3 years. Hardly ever spoke to her for more than

5 seconds at a time. So I see her at a bar all alone and I sit at her table. We got to talking and drinking, she looks beautiful and I couldn't possibly be more in love with this girl.

Then she starts talking about her new implants. Bang! My pinga hits the bottom of the table. That was funny because she turned to her left then to her right, and said, "Did you hear that?"

I guess I *could* be more in love.

Once she started slurring her speech, I thought, *OMG, I might actually get this chick.*

For guys, we're never sure if we're gonna have sex. It's not up to us. If we go out with you, just take it for granted that we *want* to have sex with you.

Then she laid it on me, "I'm a 23-year-old virgin."

Now, my common sense side says, "Okay, forget it. A girl like this is not going to let you be first.

But my pinga side was a lot more optimistic, "Give her anything she wants, I want to be her first." He was saying that as he was eating his way through my zipper.

So finally she says, "Let's go back to my place." Then she fell off her bar stool. That's always a good omen; me and my pinga high-fived each other that this might just happen. Now we're back to the Froot Loop part. I mean, it just would *not* go in. I was chiseling these memories in granite in my mind.

Finally, I broke through. The first stroke, "I love you baby."

Second stroke, "I'm making love to a goddess."

Third stroke, "Oh shit."

The fourth stroke was a bunch of apologies interrupted only by the snores of my sleeping pinga.

Guys, even a virgin knows bad sex when she's having it. I never saw her again. And that's why I now hate Froot Loops.

———

You know, a lot of people come to see my act for my misaligned but truthful views of American sex. For the moment, let's take a look at the common masturbator. But not too close, he'll shoot your eye out.

Sorry, I love that movie. Is it wrong for me to assume that most of these creatures are men? I think there are only 2 reasons a woman would masturbate:

1) You're either cute and you're caught up in the moment, or 2), you're a human wreck with no confidence. You can't be *that* bad. I just heard about 3 guys that had sex with the same watermelon. Now I'm sure one of these guys would be more than happy to take your raggedy old scootch out for a joyride.

For guys, we only have one reason to tickle the pickle. We can't get laid. When we can, we do. I've walked away from 3 jobs just for some midafternoon sex. And it's not like I slipped out the back door and didn't say anything. I walked into my boss's office and said, "My girlfriend just texted me so I'm going home to fuck her for a while but I'll be back by 2…2:30 tops."

You'd be amazed how many bosses think that's not a valid excuse to go home. They all fired me. I bet they were all masturbators that were jealous of my sexual success. Who cares if I can't get a job and live on welfare? I don't have callouses all over my pinga.

But I'm not telling you folks anything you don't already know. Even the media knows and they're the last to pick up on anything.

I can prove it. When you go home tonight turn on your TV and run through your channels, you're bound to find a 1-900 sex line channel; you will know you've hit it when you see the skank licking a lollipop asking for you to call her. And in fine print in the bottom corner, it will read, "Only $3.95 per minute."

I get it but I don't get it. She talks dirty to you, got it. Now where is the guy? Are you in the bathroom or in the bedroom? Are you wearing a third sock or has your Serta mattress become an *In*serta mattress?

Well, I don't know. It's not like I can go up to strangers on the street and ask them, "Excuse me you're pretty fucked up looking. I'll bet you masturbate a lot. How do you do it?" *Sounds like a career without a future.*

Those sex line commercials should put a little truth in advertising: "For the best piece of ass you can give yourself, call 1-900-YOU-LOSER."

And for those of you who don't know, I'm starting a campaign to get men to shake hands using their left hand. I'm tired of feeling that crazy callous in their right hand. Now it may not be all of them, some may dig ditches with a shovel; others may make sausage for a living. But other guys, and you *know w*ho you are, please get some skin moisturizer for your hand…anti-bacterial if they have it.

And another thing, there are no 1-900 commercials for women. There's no blonde-haired German guy saying, "Hello, my name is Hans. Would you like me to release my shi-stooker from my lederhosen? If so, call me now at 1-900-BIG-DICK.

I think men and women have different ideas of how the other masturbates. When guys think about women doing it, we think of beautiful women we know or have met. We wouldn't think about an ugly woman, otherwise we'd go back to our ex-wives.

So, beautiful women taking a bubble bath with candles lit and the Barry White CD running. It's always Barry White. Do his deep quivering vocals do something that makes it better?

It's that deep vibrating, "OOOOhh, yeah baby!"

Speaking of vibrating, guys, did you know if you stick your junk in a saxophone and play it, your junk will grow up to 3 inches longer? Yeah…that's a lie. I just invested in a saxophone factory and I'm trying to promote some sales so f-ing shoot me.

So...we have girl, tub, candles and Barry. Then a few gentle strokes until mind and body become one. Am I close?

And guys think a woman believes a guy doing it looks like a monkey furiously tugging at the ripcord of a faulty parachute...

Ladies, you are closer than you think.

The next time you two, you know, knock it out and you want to freak him out, ask who he was thinking about tonight? You will see a flash of terror race across his face, "Oh my god, she knows. She can read my mind. How long has this been going on?"

———

I don't think I'm a good parental role model for my kids.

I came home from a date and my son asked me how it went. I said everything went just like I planned; we had a great meal, got loaded and enjoyed incredible sex in her Corvette. But she's just a fuck-buddy, son. They are great to have, don't get me wrong, but it's not love.

For about 3 seconds I thought that maybe I should not have been so blatantly honest with my son. Then I thought, OMG, maybe I'm starting to mature. Luckily that was a passing thought.

Know what I think? I think every dad would like to be with his son when he's nailing his first girl: For guidance, if for nothing else…and to relive his youth.

And I think every guy with a daughter couldn't stand to be there the first time, watching his little princess get mauled by some pimply faced little dweeb who will awkwardly stab at his daughter's body till one thrust finds its way home.

I think that's why a lot of men who have daughters have male pattern baldness. It's not genetics, they're yanking it out. Yup, it's always better to be a father of a stabber then a stabbee.

You know when I was a kid I used to nail some farmer's daughter. And he had shotguns...lots of shotguns. I was very, very careful when and where I fucked this guy's daughter.

He told me the first time we met, "If you try to fuck my daughter, you'll be shitting lead for a month."

I had quite a dilemma. I love a good challenge, but she did have a set of knockers that made old men like me cry. Luckily, I was 14 at the time. I thought all boobs were perfect...they're not.

And then there was this whole "being shot" thing. It's not like it was the first time I'd been shot. And shotguns are for people who can't shoot. I may take a few pellets but, that's it, nothing I won't laugh about later...you know, unless I don't hear him and I feel the barrel making itself comfortable up my ass.

Here's the scenario. Depending on how much he loves his daughter, the BEST I can hope for is to be raped by the gun barrel. I think the smart move would be to beg this guy for his daughter's hand.

But that's if you wanna live. You may have an epiphany that life will never get better than that very moment, so you say, "Now, I'm going to go bang your wife." In 3 seconds, you'll be beef jerky.

Chapter 5:
I Love You, But Get Out

I don't think women understand why guys lie to them.

Ladies, it's because you hate the truth. You ask us about things you don't really want to know. So we start out telling the truth and then halfway in, because of your facial expressions, we keep adjusting the story with a few…lies.

After we are done, it's a house of cards we hope you soon forget. I gotta tell you about this chick that shanghai'd me.

Let me set the mood… It was a beautiful day, I guess around noon; just a day full of potential. I was with a beautiful girl and my only thought was where was I going to make love to this girl next?

She turned to me and said, "Honey, have you ever been with 2 women at one time?"

I swear, the birds stopped chirping and there was a clap of thunder on a bright and sunny day.

So me, thinking about hot sweaty sex and thinking with the wrong freaking head, blurts out, "No, but—"

All of a sudden, the good head grabs the handbrake and slams the tongue into the 'off' position. But it was too late…and I swear I saw a little twinkle in her eye.

"But…but what, honey?"

Now, you can't go back in time but you can hit her with a "You don't wanna know." So you can run the story through your mind just to see how it sounds. And yes, she *did* wanna know.

So I said, "Well, I had 3 different women in one day." That was a lie because it was really 4. But even I thought that sounded whoreish.

But without the "you don't wanna know," I would have said 4. So basically, it's the truth with a minor discrepancy. But by the look on her face I had a lot of repair work to do. Then the scrambling of lies began.

"Uh, uh, it was the summer solstice, the longest day of the year. Uh, I was drunk…uh, I think I hit one girl twice…uh, and one session was a blowjob."

I can flap away just about anything. She stopped listening to me when I said 3. That's what she's still thinking about. And now the day is ruined and it's my fault. "Why are you giving me the finger? You're the one who asked."

Another thing women like to do to us is a little thing I call 'entrapment.' I fall into that hole each and every time. Same scenario, slightly bigger girl.

Pleasant day, we're getting dressed, then, "Sweetheart, do I look fat?"

And my response was a solid, "Uh, no."

The answer was correct but the delay with the 'uh' somehow made it wrong. When her annunciation with the "T" in fat is first audible my 'no' should have been flying from my lips.

The fact that I gave the question the slightest inkling of thought made me wrong…and I got "the look" that she knew I was lying. But again, don't ask questions you don't want to know the answer to. If you're fat or out of shape, you know it.

Then she took a deep breath and hit me with some of that sub-human woman speed talks:

"youtookawhiletoanswerdoyoureallythinki'mfat youknowIhardlycastashadowi'mindoublesizesist hiswhywedontgooutanymoredoyouthinki'msom esortofobeseswamphog?"

"I'm sorry honey, I was locked into the game. Did you say something?"

Why are you giving me the finger again?

———

I'm seeing a woman now who's allergic to flowers. Do you have any idea how much cash I save just from not having to buy flowers? And *that* was from design.

I looked for a girl allergic to flowers on purpose. There was a flower store in the mall and as soon as you smelled it, you had to go in and she walked by the store like she was strolling through a leper colony.

I used the flower shop as bait. Once I had her hooked, I followed her for 3 days. And she had no idea. I tailed her to a Chinese buffet. That won her a lot of points.

After that, she went to a bar. I know I was there. She knew how to work a beer bottle too. She'd pound 2, then leave. This showed the makings of an excellent designated driver which gave her more points.

Apparently she must have begun to notice me. She came around the bush and said, "When the fuck are you going to talk to me?"

She knew she was being _____. Who wouldn't be?

Well, now I'm in love. And we're not even introduced.

I asked her out, she accepted, and here we are. But don't tell her. She might think that's creepy. I told her a completely different story that she was more than happy to accept.

I have a pretty good idea that most women don't like being hunted...I uh, mean, screened without their knowledge. It's actually not that bad of a system, though, because nobody gets hurt, because nobody is in a relationship. All of a sudden somebody pops out of the background and says, "I think we'd be happy together."

If I was single, I don't think I would mind being hunted by some love-struck cutie pie. As long as she doesn't look like a possum, I'd be happy.

I'm at that age where I'm thinking about my future.

Not financially, heavens NO! I'm buddying up to people just for the fact that someday I may need someone to wipe my ass. You have got to really be in someone's good graces to have them wipe your ass when you can't.

Of course, that's if I'm not married…again. If I am, she has to be cute with a nice ass, just in case I'm the wiper. You don't mind so much then.

But I was in a relationship recently where she had a horrible ass. There was like half a dozen asses on one girl and I had to escape. The thought of having to stick my hand anywhere near these…asses…scared me. I couldn't see it happening, so my subconscious crow barred me from the relationship. *Thank you, Mr. Subconscious.*

Did that ever happen to you? You're in a relationship and it just doesn't seem like its working? So the day you're thinking about ending it, your better half ends it first. That has got to be one of the greatest feelings there is, it is right there…just under orgasms.

And as long as you're not like some loser that wonders why she dumped you, this is just perfect.

She: "You don't have to leave just now."

Me: "No, no, let me grab my clothes and shit and I'll leave…and thank you. This is just so fuckin perfect. You really made my day. No, my year. Thank you."

I think in most cases women like to see their ex's down, if not crying. When you thank them, they seem stunned.

She: "Well, what do you mean by that?"

Me: "That means I'm free to go out and bang women I wanna bang. So, thank you."

You may want to back up a few steps to get out of kick range. When you say something like that to your girl, a kick in the cookies is like a knee jerk reaction. *(Excuse the pun)* Sometimes I can see taking the shot to the balls because instantly your good mood is over.

That 12 seconds from when she lets you go till you utter that fateful line is like the sun just came crashing through and you want to live again. By the 13th second, a dark cloud appears and as you're pondering that cloud on the horizon knowing something bad is about to happen... Half a second later you're on the ground coughing up blood and semen wondering why she would kick you. Strange, huh?

So why wouldn't you back up? Because that golden 12 seconds of incredible happiness is like a treasure you store in a chest in your mind. And since most of us will only live moments like these a handful of times, you need them. You can crack open these chests of happiness every once in a while and relive the moment like a past glory. You can actually feel its warmth.

Are you still following me? Okay, let's press on.

Now if you just talk things out and decide splitting is best, it's kind of anti-climactic. But don't get me wrong, it still feels good. But the moment's not there…you *want* the moment.

If the relationship just crumbles till one of you decides never to go home, there's just no glory there. A lot of unnecessary suffering because neither of you have the balls to say, "Get out."

Listen to me. You *want* that relationship moment. It's better than the feeling you have in a marriage when the 'divorce' word first pops up. Don't get me wrong, that's a great feeling too, but divorce is like 2 boxers that just went 12 rounds. You don't care who won, you just want to get out of there.

I better change the subject. Somebody out there might start thinking I make a lot of sense. Next thing you know, I'm being sued in court for instigating a divorce.

Dude: "But your honor, he told me to."

———

It's all about respect. There is no respect anymore.

I think the chain of respect combined with the decline of the English language is almost as low as it can get right now.

Last Christmas my 8-year-old grandson opened the present I gave him while I was in the pool room kicking ass and denting a keg with my bottomless kidneys.

After a couple minutes, he walked in to thank me. He must have forgotten what I got him because he said, "Thank you grand pop for that, uh, fucking thing."

I had a drunk déjà vu moment, which is a lot better than a déjà vu moment straight. You really feel like you've accomplished something when you realize where you remember the first time something happened.

And the moment was that my son said the exact same thing to my dad on his 8th Christmas.

———

My dad and 2 uncles died a few years apart and there was a time when we were all young.

We were in the midst of a boring family get-together when my dad told me he was going to the store for a minute. 5 minutes later, I saw one of my uncles slip out the back door. A moment later, the other uncle stepped out for a smoke and he was gone.

6 hours later I found them wasted away at the bar around the corner. When my dad saw me coming, he smiled and said, "This is a life lesson. Always remember it. And don't tell your mom where we are."

Now I figure they're all fucked up together in Heaven waiting for me to walk in. "Here's to you fellas!"

Love you, Dad.

———

My mom made a general statement last year that stuck in my head. I can't help but feel she now gets her opinions from 'The View', or some other female jibber-jabber show. I have nothing against jibber-jabber, but sometimes I

think they just love to hear their own voices:
Content not important.

I said, "I was walking in the woods and saw a large bunch of deer."

My mom said, "Be careful. It's mating season."

So I looked at her. "Come *on* Mom, it'd have to be a really big deer before I became its bitch."

She said, "No, I think it's the female deer that are dangerous."

So I thought about that for a moment; cute little fuzzy white tailed deer are going to aggressively rub their crotches up against my pinga? Out in the woods, miles away from anyone? Would I be able to run away from that? Of course, it would be better if they were human, but if I was forced...

If it happens I would sacrifice myself for you folks. Think of the material I'd get from that for you guys to enjoy. Oh look, a *real* woodie!

So I looked at my mom and said, "Let's talk about something else." I like talking to my mom. She's fun to talk to but…

Chapter 6:
Conglomafux III: The
Corruption of Hell

You know what the great thing about being immature is? Not only do you think about ways to improve your world, you actually do it… And I don't mean take a class and get a better job.

I'm thinking more like when you're in a restaurant and a baby won't stop crying, and the parents are deaf to it so they just let it continue. They expect someone else to discipline their child, so why not you?

I bring a wide rubber band and flick peas at the little bastard's head. They don't know what's going on so they shut up for a minute to think about it.

The satisfaction one gets at shutting up someone else's kid with a pea shot to the back of the head…you just feel so good, like standing outside naked on a windy day kind of good.

It's a pride only someone really immature can understand. You controlled him like a marionette. I don't like shooting at little girls. It's been my experience that when they get hit with a pea they scream louder. The pitch of a screaming female baby can bust glasses and eardrums.

One time a waitress asked me if there was anything else I wanted. I asked her to go backhand a kid.

She didn't. I think that showed really *poor* customer service.

It's usually the child of rich snooty parents who bother me. "Money is the root of all evil. The opposite of evil is good. I'm good, hence, I have no money and most of the people I know who have money are basically evil."

That is a quality saying.

Now a saying like, "Money can't buy happiness," has got to be the stupidest combination of 4 words you'll ever see.

I'd like to try an experiment if I may. I need a volunteer. Someone that truly believes that money doesn't buy happiness. I will take said volunteer to a town they've never been to before located 500 miles away. I will take all your money and anything valuable you happen to be wearing. You stay within the town limits for a week. GO!

I'll bet the average person would be squealing by day 4.

Me: "Hey man. You don't look so good."

Volunteer: "I've been eating dumpster food and sleeping in the woods."

Me: "Gee, that's too bad. Say, is that a new limp you're sporting?"

Volunteer: "Yeah. I got bit by a snake last night and the doctor won't do anything if I can't pay him."

Me: "So you need money for anti-venom?"

Volunteer: "Yes."

Me: "And anti-venom would bring you happiness?"

Volunteer: "Yes, yes, yes…now give me some freaking money."

Me: "I came up with 2 sayings about your recent adventures. Which one do you like better? 'Poverty buys unhappiness' or 'Money does buy happiness.'"

Volunteer: "Fuck you."

Me: "I'll strike that in my win column. Thank you for playing along."

———

Another myth I plan to expose tonight is the one about cats having 9 lives. Did anyone happen to bring their cat tonight? Don't worry, in case this myth is an exaggeration, I'm sure that petty cash can flip you a couple bucks for, you know, a funeral.

And please feel free to not watch the show. Watching your cat possibly harmed can be very traumatic.

Sometimes we can kill 2 myths at once. You know how they're supposed to land on all 4 legs? That is not true either. If you ever threw a cat off the Empire State Building, you'd know it wasn't true.

If you know me at all, you know those are jokes...yes they are. But I'll get nasty letters from a few nuts with nothing more important to do than sit around playing with themselves, wondering who they can annoy next. So, I'm sorry...and I'm sorry for this next piece, too...

———

A friend of mine made me a challenge. He said, "I'll bet you can't find a silver lining in a slaughterhouse."

I immediately shot back, "A slaughterhouse is one big fat silver lining."

He just kind of blinked real fast...like you guys are doing now.

You're not looking at the big picture! You only see the 'Boohoo, I'm a steak' picture. Now look, if I'm a cow, a bull. A male cow's a bull, right? Alright, I'm a bull. I've been fed well all my life, had shelter from the weather, and made lots of baby cows with cool looking girl cows. A good life, but I know there's payback.

One day, every bull is gonna jump in the truck and take a ride down some dark road. And personally, when I get that cold confused feeling I'm getting laid one more time. I *know* we're not going back to the farm, so I better make the most of it.

Anyway…next thing I know, some guy with a southern accent is telling me to say hello to a Burger King…whatever that means. And that's all I remember.

Chickens are a little different. I think a rooster looks forward to death more than a bull. He just bangs chickens all day and night.

Know why a rooster is crowing at 6 every morning? His pinga hurts. That's what 'cock a doodle doo' means: "My pinga is killing me." But at 9:00 a.m. he's ready to go. "Okay ladies, let's make this a great day."

And when it's my turn on the chopping block, my sore little pinga and I will be ready to go.

See, I said there were silver linings everywhere. Sometimes, you just have to look a little deeper.

One more thing… Do you think chicken nuggets have pieces of chicken nuggets mixed into it?

So let me see if I got this right…a P.E.T.A. tries to save animals and Pita is a burrito with ground up animals?

Boy, did I go to the wrong rally. I had people chasing me with torches after that one. Those folks are c.r.a.z.y!

So I show up at this rally and I'm starving. All the little tents that served food were selling…something. It was like 'glop' over here and 'gloop' over there. A week of food like that would probably ensure never having a solid bowel movement ever again.

But as luck would have it, I remembered I had a chunk of beef jerky in my pocket. So I took to gnawing on it. Some old man came over to see what it was. As I raised it up, he got a horrified look on his face then he fainted.

At least I hope he fainted. I'd hate to think someone saw me walking away from a body that was…you know, dead. That could harm my career.

———

Another thing my career doesn't need is a drunk driving rap.

And I've been guilty of driving with 3 or 12 beers in me before. I'm really happy the people I've driven around with have good reflexes. What bothers me, are the guys who have a couple shots of tequila before going to a girl's house to have a couple shots of tequila. The guy is doing figure 8's around phone poles.

My advice is to not pop a bunch of mints and drive. Put yourself in the cop's place.

If you're a chick, a cop is thinking, "Well, with that breath her lips are going to be making some guy happy tonight." He may let you go, or go in the woods. There are ways to work these things out.

If you're a guy and your breath smells like tic-tacs…same thing. Try this, suck down an onion, a big ole soft and smelly that should have been thrown out last month, before the officer gets to the window.

"Do you want my insurance or my liCENse?"

He will wave you on. "Go, get out of here, my mistake." And he will hold his nose while waving you on.

———

I think it's about time we pay tribute to some of the old, everyday inventions we take for granted. Today, it's all about cell phones. They do everything but have sex with you. And if it has a vibrate button on it, you might have used it for that too…anybody out there want to confess anything tonight??

No? Uh, me either.

The 'greatest' invention that comes to mind right off the bat is toilet paper. Have you ever had to do this? You get done what you wanna get done and that's when you notice you're out of paper. A cold chill goes up your spine…you are trapped.

The tissue box is empty but nobody threw it out. You had the brilliant idea to take the magazine rack out of the bathroom last month because everybody spent too much time reading in there. And last, but not least, you're not wearing socks. This is now a problem.

Did you ever have to open the door a crack and yell out to someone to get you a roll? That's happened to me…a lot. Some people lose their keys…a lot. Some people don't use turn signals…a lot. I forget to check for paper…a lot.

Once it happens to me, I'll remember to look the next 3 or 4 times, but then there's always paper. Then I get lulled into a false sense of security. On the fifth or sixth time, I'll drop my guard, forget to look, and then I'm stuck again.

Last night, in a very nice restaurant, it must have been the fifth or sixth time. There I sat, all alone in a single person bathroom. I was not going to open the door a crack and yell for somebody.

The only paper in this room is the wallpaper. I thought about it for a couple seconds before I thought against it… Plus it was on too tight.

This was just one of the dilemmas. I also clogged the toilet. I didn't mean to. I had to go…a lot. And, of course, no plunger.

It was one of those nights where you sacrifice both socks and try to sneak out without being seen.

As angry as I felt about the poorly stocked bathroom, I did feel pity for the minimum wage worker who had THAT clean up job.

———

Some inventions I don't think were completed… like cottage cheese. Yuck. Did the inventor die while inventing cottage cheese and whoever found the carcass clutching the bowl of cottage cheese probably figured the invention was complete? Well, it's not. And…Yuck.

I have an idea that would make billions. You know how the government is coming up with billions of laws on driving? They have the cell phone laws; now they want a "no eating" law, "no reading the paper" law and, my favorite, "no playing with your dog while driving" law.

Your government is so concerned with your safety and well being they will ticket anybody doing *anything* stupid behind the wheel. Even you.

So my invention is giant rubber bumpers around every car. If somebody runs a red light and T-bones you, you both bounce around like some sort of pinball domino thing. Maybe 50 cars will get bumped but no one gets hurt…except the guy getting a present from his mistress…he could be seriously injured.

And if you get involved in an accident, circus music comes out of your radio. Hah, I just got a craving for cotton candy.

Some inventions inspire other inventions and the natural progression is apparent.

The fork came before the knife. Man built a fork. Some food was too big to shovel in so the knife was invented.

You see how that works? Let's see if you can figure out which invention preceded the other. Okay, here you go. The coke, or the coke spoon? Come on, people. This is drug class 101.

My god, it's so obvious. It's coke, people. Nobody invented a coke spoon and then said, "I wish someone would invent something called coke so I could use my spoon."

The answer is coke. Someone invented cocaine, put it in a bag and said, "How do I get the coke from my bag to my nose? I got it! I'll invent the coke fork. 20 minutes later, a painful nose and a lot of spilled cocaine, and the coke spoon was invented.

————

I think scientists should be inventing a pill you take if you would like to grow rabbit fur all over your body.

Don't you think that would feel great? And sex would probably feel incredible. You might have to lessen the 8 hour work day back to 6 hours. That would probably help keep absenteeism down.

One pill and your life would change forever. If you take a second pill, either your crank falls off or the happy hole seals up. Graphic enough for you? And of course, it's not true, but would you risk it?

I'll bet fat people would really be in demand. So big and cuddly. *What?* You're offended by the word 'fat'? Would you prefer I say "height challenged" people? What are you

bitchin about? You're not even fat; I'd say
you're chunky…

Now what are you pissed off about? Do you
fight the fight of the fat people? You stand up
for them because they can't stand up for
themselves…because they're fat. Look lady, I
love fat people. Most are very friendly and they
keep me warm in the winter.

What does that mean? How the hell do I
know? I was talking about rabbit fur and you
distracted me. A lot of people are tired of
political correctness and I will lead that war.
Look at this picture on my phone. See that? That
is a *Christmas* tree not a *holiday* tree.

I'm sorry about that tangent, folks. I hate
being heckled. Know what being heckled is
like? It's like, if I followed that lady to the
whorehouse she works at and slapped the pinga
right out of her mouth. That is what being
heckled is like.

Back to rabbit fur. And let's hope there is
no "male pattern fur baldness." I don't know if

that would be a good look for guys. It's not like you can just shave that problem away. I mean, where would you stop? People would start thinking you have a bad case of mange.

OH MY GOD… OMG, right? OMG, since we're on the subject of fur I have to tell you guys something. I went over to a friend's house and my friend's sister came over and she brought her cat…the cat was furless…no fur. It's the new, hot breed.

It was the ugliest thing I ever saw. And the cat was worse. I love that joke.

No, but seriously, I had a hard time looking at it. I also felt bad for it. And I said to her, "Why would you buy such an ugly cat?"

She said, "He's not ugly, he's furless. I'm allergic to fur."

So I said, "Why not get something else?"

And she said, "But he's cuddly."

Yuck. So I said, "Snakes are cuddly too and they're furless."

WAIT…a snake covered in fur. Take away the sick sexual undertones and that would make a pretty cool pet. Give *him* a pill also.

———

That's no crazier than some southern folks I've met. They are bull headed. But I mean that in a nice way. After the last crop of tornados devastated the south, it always amazed me that they'll clean up what's left of their trailer homes; they'll have a new one put on the same exact cinderblocks. Not even a thought about moving like say…north. They interviewed this one good ole boy and it went like this:

Interviewer: "So this is your house or what's left of it?"

Jimbob: "Yup, it's all gone. But I found my recliner a ways up the road yonder. And would you believe it, the dang thing still works."

Interviewer: "Is this the first house you lost to a tornado?"

Jimbob: "Hell no, this is the third one in ten years."

Interviewer: "I knew it. I interviewed you when you lost your house to another tornado last year."

Jimbob: "You're wrong, Mr. Microphone fella. I lost that house to a hurricane."

Interviewer: "You are just a lucky guy, Jimbob."

———

The summer of 2012 will be remembered as a real hot one. There was a drought everywhere. The newscasters were talking about failed crops and sky-rocketing produce. That scared the hell out of me so I took action. I called my dealer and told him to put a pound of weed off to the side for me…for all those warm chilly nights when I can't get to sleep… Droughts a drought man.

But I knew it was coming. It's the year of the Armageddon. If the devil is walking the planet now, you have to figure he's going to crank up the heat.

You see, the devil lives in hell and hell is like fire. What did it feel like walking out your front door this morning? Fucking fire.

It's always about facts, folks. I'm like a German Charlie Chan. The Armageddon cranks me up. Bet you never heard anybody say that before.

But they come up with all these survival guides. What to do and where to go. Where to go is the one that gets me. Head to Pigblossom, Missouri. There's nothing there but stills.

Well, I'm suspicious already. If I can read "Pigblossom, Missouri" in a book, then a terrorist can read it, too. And then I'm supposed to be lured there by moonshine. It sounds too good to be true so I'll bet a terrorist wrote that book.

Matter of fact, it also said, "If you can't find fresh water, you can drink urine straight from the faucet." I'd have to be *really* thirsty before I get to that point. *Really!*

It also said, you can live pretty happily off rat meat. I may be able to live off it…but not happily. Bet they have some little ass drumsticks, huh? I heard it's a delicacy in other post-apocalyptic countries.

A little catsup and a tight blindfold and it tastes just like chicken made from rat meat.

You know, in a couple years from now you're going to be out with your rat hunting posse, trying to escape the deadly rays of the sun and remember these jokes and you're going to laugh. Then you're gonna say, "I should have killed that bastard…THERE! A rat!"

And the TV shows are worse. I kid you not; a survivalist killed an elk, cut out its asshole, and ate it. Then he looked into the camera and said, "If I could eat that, you could surely eat the rest." Now *that's* a man who made his point.

That's giving 100%.

These people that say, "I gave 110%." NO…70% at best. It's when you're eating an asshole to make a point that you've finally reached 100%.

I know I keep saying it might be a nuclear war, but the Earth may get us too. Suppose it stops spinning really quick… Just stops. And we're all flung into space toward Saturn. There's only going to be a handful of us holding a pound of weed under our arms. We may run out of air but I'll find something to breathe.

I think the knowledge that when I burn through my pound and I'm out of stuff to breathe may keep me from fully enjoying my buzz.

———

I like making up games in my mind. And the next day, I come up with another.

Last Friday's game was, "If you can bitchslap anyone in history, who would you backhand?" That was a fun game. I brought that one up on stage at my show.

My answer was simple. Joan of Arc. A good backhand across her noggin would have probably saved her life. "We all have that little voice in our heads… It's not God…Whack."

You never know, she may have borne an important child. This is what I would probably have said to her. "When they start walking you toward the stake, stop talking about how God told you he'd destroy their armies…Whack."

You see, this is fun.

The first guy I asked said, "Christopher Columbus." He also said he was half American Indian. The funny thing is, the other half is Italian. I wonder if he's tormented. He said he made his choice. He probably has outrageous psychiatrist bills also.

I had a couple people tell me "Adolf Hitler" and it was for 2 different reasons.

The first guy just liked the small moustache look and now it was ruined.

The second guy had a better reason. His grandfather died during WWII. He fell down the stairs at the induction center and broke his neck.

I hope being dead doesn't suck. …And I really hope once you go where you go that moustache look is optional.

———

Does it bother any of you that cameras are everywhere? In fast food stores, on traffic lights, even my headboard. Yeah, there have been some real crimes in my bed. I've had my innocence stolen there. I've had my house swiped from me. though some people call that a "fair divorce" settlement.

But do folks care about being filmed? I don't care, you know, unless I'm drunk. Then I can see cause for concern. I've tried to function in public a few times when I was out of my mind and it did not go well.

Do you think cameras are really the answer? Bring back corporal punishment; snap a few limbs that will get the sour underbelly of society back in line.

How about changing some signs a bit? How about, "Violators will be prostituted." Let the criminals figure it out.

And how about signs that are helpful? "Speed limit: 65 but we ticket after 69." That one would have saved me lots of money. I really thought we had a 20mph cushion.

There are all kinds of ways to stop crime. But the MAN doesn't want you to know. Did that sound historic but fresh?

Okay, way #1. Everybody wears police uniforms. Would you buy weed from a dude wearing a uniform? I get nervous enough buying it from dudes wearing "Macho Comacho Lives" t-shirts.

#2: Arm *everybody*. That's right; give anybody who wants a gun, a gun. Can't get the criminals guns then arm anyone that wants to hunt them…ohuh, I mean protect ourselves. It could work.

Suppose one day we all wake up and there was no religion. Would the world burst out in chaos? Oh, don't mind me. I'm just standing here trying to kick-start Armageddon. She sure is taking a long time getting here.

And that's why I drink so much. If I wake up in hell I want a strong enough hangover not to care. See, a lot of people don't think about these things.

Your average sober soul will be begging and crying not to be tortured. My soul will be like, "Give it your best shot. I have 50 bucks that says you can't break me."

When I talk about such things it drives the religious fanatic's nuts. It's like, saying Armageddon and all of a sudden God and the devil will remember they're supposed to be fighting for all our souls and then we get mixed up in it. That's not supposed to be too pleasant. My retirement plans at this time are as follows.

If I die instantaneously, I have no plan. It's been taken care of.

If I live, I'll sell all my possessions and bet on the outcome of Armageddon. I could end up a very rich man during the post-apocalyptic clean-up. I'll get that nice little cabin in the mountains with a valley where I can pick off zombies for a thousand years. I just hope they're the slow zombies. I don't know who came up with fast zombies, but they suck.

I like my zombies slow and stupid. I want them baffled by a chain link fence. Then they'll turn and go eat my neighbor. And if the zombies are slow enough I'll even run over and open the neighbor's gate for them... Hey, it's not like he's a *good* neighbor.

I do have a medical question I need answered if anybody out there is qualified to answer it.

Okay, I'm a zombie and I resort to cannibalism. Do fat people really have a lot more carbs than a person in good shape? I figure I'd ask now while I can. You know, zombies can't talk...so I'm asking now.

I think if I become a zombie and there's the slightest speck of my personality in my carcass, I'd be going after the women. I just don't think I'd be happy eating 'guy' meat. Even if it's just the brain that we eat, I'd still feel funny doing it to a dude.

And what hack writer came up with that gem? "Zombies eat brains." There's not an animal out there that targets the brain as a food supply. So what are we being told here, folks? The minute we die and become the undead we get a craving for brains? That sounds like corporate B.S. if you ask me.

———

If zombies don't get us it doesn't matter. People are mutilating *themselves*.

Why are so many people getting body piercings lately? Having metal invade your body, I don't get it. I was accidentally stabbed one time and I didn't like. I think it was an accident…he said it was.

I was being mugged, and this dude stabbed me when I wouldn't give up my ring. I know it happened right after I told him to go fuck himself…maybe that had something to do with it.

When I didn't go down I shot him a really mean look. I think he realized he made a mistake when I jumped on his body and broke it. His body, that is…oops.

Here's a strange thing: If a guy gets a nipple pierced, I can't look at it…too gross…but if it's a girl, no problem. It doesn't bother me. It's not gross and I can look at it all day.

I've seen worse. I've seen pierced genitalia. My question is, why? Is sex so bad with you that you have to spice it up by putting shiny things on it…like a fishing lure? I couldn't imagine.

I can imagine when the piercing gun goes off and I jump; I can see myself really fuck myself up. I'd be running down the road screaming for a pair of pliers.

I don't know why people want to walk around in pain. I went to this one freak fest where this guy was wearing a clamp on his head that was so tight, it was changing the shape of his skull.

I asked him if it hurt, and he said, "Yeah…a lot."

Then why do it? Again, it must be me. I wonder what theories scientists will come up with a thousand years from now when they find his head in an archaeological dig. I think all those UFO nuts will have all the evidence they need with his skull.

———

There are other ways to amuse yourself. Invent a game…any game.

Here's the sickest game I ever played.

My father is dead. He's been that way a number of years now.

On the third anniversary, I earned money for it. I was stuck in a job I hated and I showed up for work with red eyes…redder than usual. I was upset.

As I walked to the time clock, my boss walked over to me and said, "Your eyes are red, Mr. Morgan. Have we been drinking this morning?"

What I wanted to say was, "Go fuck yourself." What I actually said was, "My father died today." I broke down before I could finish saying, "Three years ago."

Well, his jaw dropped, "My *god*, Buffalo. Take the next couple days off with pay. You didn't have to come in today."

All of a sudden that little bell went off in my head: "Ding!" Acting 101. "I was afraid to ask for Friday off so I could go to the funeral."

Now my boss is crying, "I had no idea you were such a dedicated employee. Take the *whole* week off."

Now that was a good week. Thanks Pop.

Nice game.

———

Let's go back to a quieter, gentler time. Let's talk about liquor and women without morals.

I was at a wedding reception last summer, hell if I know who they were. I was only there for the beer. One of the bridesmaids was just gorgeous. A little loud…yes; a little obnoxious…yes. A lot drunk…yes, yes.

That's the kind of girl you want to see drink lots of tequila. She is only going to get wilder. I don't drink too much before…you know… sex. That, "this never happened before" thing might happen again.

Okay, that's right. It happened to me, okay. Back in high school there I was, naked, with the girl of my dreams, begging me to make her eyeballs spin like pinwheels. I had one hand on a piece of silly string I usually call my pinga and the other was clutching a trash can painting like a giant coke can that I was puking schnapps into. *Ladies, it is very hard to do both at the same time so show a little mercy.*

And…puking will take priority because otherwise we wouldn't puke. We'd be too busy making rug burns and blisters. Isn't it funny how you don't feel rug burns and blisters as you're making them? You know it's gonna hurt tomorrow but you don't care today.

Is it also funny how you can go into your bedroom and it's so cold you jump under the covers; then you grab each other's fun parts and in 5 minutes, you're kicking off the covers?

Where was I? Oh, yeah, the insane chick.

She had this one talent that was great. I loved it. But after about 22 hours of it the novelty started to wear off. I finally cracked while eating a pizza. I said those 3 words I never thought I'd say to a woman, "STOP BLOWING ME."

So she bit me. Jokes on her, she chipped a tooth. *Big, strong pinga.*

Getting back to the bridesmaid…

We were having a great time in the empty closet we found. She was really into it until she passed out. Now, my question is, is it wrong that I kept going till I was done? Some people I've told that to say it was wrong, some say no.

We did go out a couple times afterward and she said she didn't care. I also found out that getting drunk and passing out during sex was her M.O., so we didn't last. It's not a crime.

Thank god. I'm terrible with lawyers.

———

I shop for my lawyers at the dollar store. They are disbarred attorneys, sure, but they like to keep in practice.

The last lawyer I got there was snorting lines of coffee creamer off the dollar store employee's picnic table.

I interviewed 5 lawyers that day and Phil was the best. I forget the others, but I do remember one lawyer kept offering to do "favors" for me, and it wasn't the chick lawyer. I don't think these "favors" would have helped my case.

My best friend said, "Well, why don't you just stay out of trouble?"

I can't. My brain won't let me. Here's a few typical thoughts and observations my mind rolls out to me every day:

It's been a great year for Ford and Chevy. I've never seen so many dead deer on the side of the road...hell if I know about their sales.

They opened a new business in my neighborhood: Wong Lee's Driving Academy. Am I a racist if this worries me?

Is it wrong to let your children watch porn instead of answering their stupid little questions about sex?

Does my bottle of water come straight from the stream and, if so, do they check it for moose urine before packaging?

The fastest way to a woman's heart is to tell her, "Your ass doesn't look fat in those jeans."

How many people need to know who you are for you to be considered famous?

To save plastic they made the lid smaller on my bottled water but now it's considered a choking hazard. Positive or Negative?

_____

One thing in life I've learned is always be near a toilet if you're gonna play with laxatives. You don't want to be coughing in traffic squeezing your butt cheeks till they're blue. TRUTH!

So how many of you would run a red light to avoid shitting your pants? I mean a 'just turned red' light. The mental calculator comes out for the 2 seconds you're deciding whether to run it or not. "Camera might catch me for a $100 ticket or I could just sit here and shit in my $30 jeans…I'm going for it."

Did you ever poop for so long you had to catch your breath? Or you were afraid it might clog the toilet? That's usually over at someone else's house when you worry about that. If it takes a dozen flushes…it takes a dozen flushes. You just have to chisel it down. It'll go.

I've always been a fan of the outhouse. Once it leaves your body, it's gone for good. Unless the thing collapses and you fall in...you'll probably never see what you just did. And that makes some guys sad. A 3 foot poop snake might be the only thing they accomplish and talk about for the next 50 years.

Did I ever tell you about the great poop snake of "67?"

"I will f-ing kill you."

———

Ever jump into your car with the attitude: "I know this is a thousand dollar P.O.S. but I will kick your tractor trailer ass if you get in my way." There are times when that attitude is just out of whack. That's a good way to get shot.

Did you ever think about that? Getting shot while driving? That's the kind of shit they teach us in acting school. Director comes out: "Okay, *you*, I want you to drive like a real asshole and show us what happens if someone shoots you...GO."

I am speaking and my brain is narrating.

Me: "Yeah man, I'm gonna drive like a jerk-off and try to win the nightly "Silly Prick Award.""

Brain: "Is that like the Oscar?"

Me: "I'm gonna cut this guy off."

Brain: "Fuck you, dude."

Me: "Holy shit, is that a gun?"

Brain: "Holy shit, that's a gun." *Bang Bang Bang.*

Me: "I've been shot to death…"

Brain: "No, but this tree will kill us…"

CRASH.

Brain: "Now we're dead, jerk off."

Know what the director said? "Interesting." Then he gave me a business card for his therapist.

———

Camping relaxes my mind. I was thinking about going camping next spring. I got lost from the group last time I went camping for almost 19 hours. Yeah, real scary. Luckily I had my survival kit on me. That includes 2 beers, a joint, and 5 pounds of beef jerky…oh, and the last of my blow. Come to think of it I was really very happy out there. I didn't want to be found.

I can't do it like that anymore. I'm more likely to go to a Holiday Inn near some woods. That way I can go hiking the next day to fix my hangover. To hell with those 'drink in the woods till you pass out' parties; you wake up with a sore back, sore neck and a tick farm roaming throughout your body.

Man, I hate ticks…they remind me of lawyers. I love screwing with lawyers. Not all lawyers. Just the scumbags…and you *know* who you are.

———

Lawyer: "I paid a half-million to educate myself but my client in the blood-soaked clothes is innocent cause he says so."

Okay, good. You believe he's innocent. How bout this? If he's found guilty, you go to jail with him. That will stop some of the silliness. I think once a year you should be able to ask a convict doing a lot of years in prison if he wants to continue serving his time or take a bullet in the back of the head. I'll bet they would clear out a few cells every year. Of course, they'd be full again in twenty minutes.

Yeah, America has a lot of criminals. And not all of them are behind bars. Look at our government. That's right, bitches. We're not all as stupid as you think, although some do show it.

One of these knuckleheads was banging a mistress and paying her $5000 a month rent…with taxpayer money. When he got busted at his house, he's standing there like Ralph Kramden, "Humina Humina Humina."

So with a mountain of evidence against him and a government lawyer, they find a jury that lets him go. Unfreakin believable.

Lawyers really have to be able to bullshit on the fly. I'm good at that, but my soul and morals would make a terrible lawyer.

———

You ever go to party and someone you apparently know but don't remember strikes up a conversation you must have started 20 years before? He might feed you a clue in the first sentence but that's all the help you get. You know you're not locked in, right?

There *are* outs.

You can try to fake your half of the conversation and hope it all clicks in a moment or two. Or, you can say, "Who the hell are you?" Who the hell are you is a little rude but easier on the brain. And 98% of the time…that's my out.

When I go with the fake out, I regret it immediately.

Last month, I'm at a barbeque in Texas and a guy comes up to me I don't remember at all. Here's why I didn't use this out.

Dude: "Hey Buff. It's been a while. Whatever happened that night your cousin had a bag of acid and we were all gonna go drag racing in the desert?"

Me: "Oh my god that was one of the greatest nights of my life."

Dude: "I don't remember it."

Me: "How could you not?"

Dude: "Because it never happened."

Now I remember him. We ditched him when he kept bugging us to stop so he could pee at McDonald's. We just left him at the urinal.

I had vague focus, but now it locked in.

Me: "You're the moronic friend of my cousin. Oh, it happened dude, but we ditched you."

You know, I'm getting too old to roll around in the dirt with my past. I'll stick with, "Who the hell are you?"

Chapter 7:
I Don't Want to be a Proctologist

You guys make a great audience but sometimes I get really bad audiences. A couple weeks ago, I had an audience I thought was going to get me killed.

In this audience, in the seat right in the middle of the room, sat this guy from one of the Arab countries. He could have passed for Italian but the robes and the turban kind of gave him away.

So I said, "Hey man, that's a nice hat."

And the audience went, "Oohhh."

Know what he said? "Thank you."

So I asked him his name and he said, "Ipey."

I said, "The bathroom's over there."

The audience "Ooww'ed" but he laughed.

Then I asked, "What do you do for a living? Anything we can talk about? I mean, is this a safe distance where I'm standing?"

The audience was stunned into silence with that one and he's laughing his ass off.

So I'm ready to get back into my show but I ask him one more time, "Ipey, what do you really do for a living?"

He has this huge smile on his face and says, "I am Senior Vice President of the Pakistan Towel Company. We make towels."

I said, "That's great. So your hat is kind of like your showroom?"

And collectively, the audience gasped. I got dizzy. Everybody sucked all the air out of the room, but Ipey fell out of his seat because he laughed so hard.

F.Y.I.? Like judges and Scotsmen, they don't wear underwear. You'd think at least he'd have worn a towel.

So when Ipey got back into his chair, I said, "Ipey, can you tell your fellow audience members to shut the fuck up?"

So he stood up and in a high pitched Indian voice said, "Shut the fuck up…this man is very funny." After that, it was a great night.

And you thought I was just another hack, huh? You folks have no idea how close your sitting to a near future…superstar. That's right. I'm just getting ready to launch my last totally reliable, sure-shot trip into the stratosphere of super stardom.

First, next Monday, I'm releasing my first celebrity porn tape, anonymously of course. Who am I with? Guess her initials were B.A.…and it wasn't Bea Arthur. Okay, it was, but she was a lot more athletic in the 70's.

Then I'm gonna join the Church of Scientology just as soon as I learn how to spell it. That's the cult that lets you have like, 10 wives, right? No, sorry, that's the Mormons. Oh, yeah, the one with the choir. I guess they *do* have a lot to sing about.

I'm surprised a celebrity hasn't become a Mormon, married a couple hotties and just rubbed it in our faces.

Johnnie Star: "Hi, you know me, everybody does. Here are my 2 wives and before you ask, yes, both of them, at the same time, every night. This is *so* much better than being a Buddhist."

And the final plan to achieve super stardom is I gotta go to rehab…I'm not sure what to go for. I don't want to go for drugs and alcohol. I have that under control and I'm not ready…

I think quitting something I'm not addicted to would be a lot easier. I was thinking something unique, like animal porn…or an obsession with the Jerry Springer show. You're right, it's pretty much the same thing.

I have to be careful of what I choose. They might want proof. I don't want to say I like sticking things up my ass, then they hand me a ladle and say, prove it.

"Hey, I'm cured. What do you know?" Maybe I'll stick with animal porn. If they force me to watch it, I suppose I can. There are worse things I could be doing.

So remember to pick up your supermarket rags this month. I hope they don't run all the stories together. It would sound like, "Buffalo Marries the Budweiser Clydesdales Before Honeymooning at the Vatican While Making a Porn Film."

The picture of me standing behind a horse with a surprised look on its face would be adorable; then a little picture of the Pope in the corner waving his bony little fist with the caption, "Pope Furious!"

———

I love comedy, folks. I had a bunch of crappy jobs before I found comedy. Painting was very therapeutic, but when I was painting I used to hear some strange things in people's homes. In one elderly couples' home, the batteries in their hearing aids must have been fried. They were in another room having an argument and I heard the whole thing:

She: "Get it in…Get it in the hole, then move up. Christ, let me do it…then move…get out of the way."

He: "Do you want to do it yourself?"

She: "Well I don't see how you're helping. I'm doing all the work. Ask the painter if he wants to help. He looks like he knows how to finish a job."

It was at this time I slipped out a dock window for coffee. I might have hung around if I'd known they were hanging curtains.

———

A friend of mine tries to get me to go to school to be a proctologist. No, thank you. That is a job I would not want. Not only do I never want to see another guy's bare ass, I sure as hell don't want to be fishing around in there.

What about if you're a repeat offender? You show up at the emergency room and your doctor, leaning on the outside of the building with a cigarette dangling from the corner of his mouth, says, "What do you have for me this week, Phil?"

See if you can guess...fart...Quack quack..." *it's a duck call.*

I salute the guys who can admit defeat; they can admit their inability to remove something by themselves so they go to the doctor. For me, if that was my 'thing', it would have to be *really* far up there. I'd try anything, laxatives...squat on a bottle of olive oil...a plunger. Start with the plunger end. If that don't work, use the handle. Go in with 2, you can chopstick the bitch out.

———

Say, do you know who the saddest slugs are?

Non-working actors and actresses are the most desperate people in the galaxy.

I went to a casting call in L.A. last year...
That's Los Angeles, sir.

So there are 50 of us losers standing around waiting for the director to show up; hold on, 49 losers and 1 guy gathering material for his comedy show…okay, 50 losers.

So this garbanzo in a cheap suit shows up and tells us what he's looking for. "Thank you for coming. I am making a Spanish snuff film this afternoon; working title, "El Snuffo." The funniest thing happened. This morning we filmed the final scene and they forgot to put film in the camera. One of the actors…uh…left the project so I need a new victim."

49 losers: "Pick me…pick me."

Director: "Okay, this is how I'm gonna choose; I'm gonna point my hand at you like a gun. When I say 'bang' give me your best 5 second death scene. Okay, *you*. Ready? BANG!"

Idiot 1: "Oh, you got me…right in the…the spleen."

Director: "Not bad but nobody knows where the spleen is. Next!"

Idiot 2: "No, what kind of gun is it?"

Director: "Uh, it's a rifle. Ready?"

Idiot 2: "But you're holding it like a pistol."

Director: "Okay, it's a handgun, ready?"

Idiot 2: "What caliber?"

Director: "What…why do you need to know that?"

Idiot 2: "Motivation."

Director: "I'm gonna circle your name. I like you. You're a real pain in the ass."

Idiot 2 to friends: "He likes me. He said I'm a real pain in the ass."

Friend of Idiot 2: "I bet you got the part."

Idiot 2: "Don't jinx me, man, don't jinx me."

Director: "You in the black hat and sunglasses. Ready? BANG!"

Me: "What are you, all fucked up?"

Director: "Did I mention if you do a good job in my film, I'll recommend they use you in next week's C.S.I.?"

49 Idiots: "OOOWWW."

Me: "Chupa the Pinga." *Already did C.S.I., chump.*

And, no, Virginia there is no Santa Claus, y'old slut.

———

I was on one of the first reality shows there ever was. And I'm still sorry about that. This led to that and that's why TV's all screwed up. Anyway, most of my appearances on the show were cut.

This is why the show was called "Scared Straight." I'm thinking just a bunch of big actors in a retired jail. It's funny to watch. In the first 5 minutes on the bus ride there, you see me a dozen times. After we step off the bus, I disappear. You see me no more. I don't even get back on the bus.

If you ever wondered what happened to me…I'll tell ya.

When we went into the first cells there was this dude who was as square and solid as a Wells Fargo bank safe, and I'm thinking, he's an actor. So I say, "Hey punk, how much more time you got?"

And he says, "53 years, asshole," as he spit every syllable in my face.

So I said, "53 years? Is that how long they gave you for fucking cows?"

He must have had a hard time believing I said that to him. It nearly took 2 seconds to try and fly through the bars to snap my neck. "I'm gonna fucking kill you man."

"Actually, your stupid ass is gonna stay right there for the next half century."

He was *really* mad. I would have hated to be his bitch that night.

But I think what got me thrown off the show was, "Hey boy, why don't you get some of your cow molesting bitches over there to help you?"

Man, there were some upset maniacs in there. S.W.A.T. was called in to get me out.

The guy running the show was yelling at me, "What the hell's the matter with you? They were going to kill you."

So I smiled and said, "He's in a cage, man. Where's he going? So I was cut. But it was a day off from school.

———

One thing I always liked doing was writing. I wrote a commercial for the N.R.A.

Okay...older guy stands on the side of the highway looking at the flat tire on his car. A young guy stops and offers to fix the man's tire. 5 minutes later, he's done and demands $20.

The older guy says no, so the younger guy steps towards him with a crowbar in his hands. The older guy draws a 38' from his jacket pocket and blows the creep's head off. Then he looks into the camera with a smile, "It's a jungle out there. Thanks N.R.A."

Then you get the anti-N.R.A. folks who want to get rid of guns with their commercials. They have a guy with a pipe, relaxing on a sofa. "I don't like guns. They scare me and hurt people. As soon as we have no more guns, we're then going after knives, dodge balls, hopes and dreams. Thank you."

I think Archie Bunker was right.

Archie: "If you wanna stop hijackings, arm all your passengers."

Miss you, Carroll.

Thank you…thank you so much. You guys were great.

Have a great night!

ABOUT THE AUTHOR

My name is Barry Hemmerle. I was a bouncer at a comedy club in the mid 1980's. Before Tim Allen broke through, we hung out together and he suggested I take a stab at comedy. After my second show, the manager thought I was good enough to M.C.

Using the name Barry Von, I worked the east coast sharpening my style of sarcastic wit. Besides jokes, I'd occasionally break beer bottles over my head or let audience members rub a spot on my temple for good luck. {It's a bullet someone put there over the beating I gave him as a teen.

A SPECIAL THANK YOU TO YOU!

On behalf of everyone at Freedom Of Speech Publishing, thank you for choosing Buffalo Morgan's Sowing the Seeds of Sanity: Sick & Funny Comedy from Buffalo's Vegas Show for your reading enjoyment.

As an added bonus and special thank you, for purchasing Buffalo Morgan's Sowing the Seeds of Sanity: Sick & Funny Comedy from Buffalo's Vegas Show, you can enjoy discounts and special promotions on other Freedom of Speech Publishing products. Visit www.freedomeofspeech.com/vip to learn more.

We are committed to providing you with the highest level of customer satisfaction possible. If for any reason you have questions or comments, we are delighted to hear from you. Email us at cs@freedomofspeechpublishing.com or visit our website at: http://freedomofspeechpublishing.com/contact-us-2/.

If you enjoyed Buffalo Morgan's Sowing the Seeds of Sanity: Sick & Funny Comedy from Buffalo's Vegas Show, visit www.freedomofspeechpublishing.com for a list of similar books
or upcoming books.

Again, thank you for your patronage. We look forward to providing you more entertainment in the future.

Buffalo Morgan's Sowing the Seeds of Sanity

Sick & Funny Comedy from Buffalo's Vegas
Show
By Barry Hemmerle

For more books like this one, visit Barry Hemmerle's
website at:
http://barryhemmerle.com/

Printed in the United States of America
The publisher offers discounts on this book when
ordered in bulk quantities. For more information,
contact Sales Department, Phone 815-290-9605,
Email:
sales@FreedomOfSpeechPublishing.com

Freedom of Speech Publishing, Leawood KS, 66224
www.FreedomOfSpeechPublishing.com

ISBN: 1938634128
ISBN-13: 978-1-938634-12-3

www.ingramcontent.com/pod-product-compliance
Lightning Source LLC
Chambersburg PA
CBHW070957040426
42443CB00007B/555